# THE GARDENER'S FRIEND

THE GARDENER'S FRIEND

Copyright © Summersdale Publishers Ltd, 2011

With research by Anna Martin

Illustrations by Kath Walker

All rights reserved.

No part of this book may be reproduced by any means, nor transmitted, nor translated into a machine language, without the written permission of the publishers.

Condition of Sale
This book is sold subject to the condition that it shall not, by way of trade or otherwise, be lent, re-sold, hired out or otherwise circulated in any form of binding or cover other than that in which it is published and without a similar condition including this condition being imposed on the subsequent publisher.

Summersdale Publishers Ltd
46 West Street
Chichester
West Sussex
PO19 1RP
UK

www.summersdale.com

Printed and bound in the UK by CPI Mackays, Chatham ME5 8TD

ISBN: 978-1-84953-152-8

---

Substantial discounts on bulk quantities of Summersdale books are available to corporations, professional associations and other organisations. For details contact Summersdale Publishers by telephone: +44 (0) 1243 771107, fax: +44 (0) 1243 786300 or email: nicky@summersdale.com.

# THE GARDENER'S FRIEND

## A MISCELLANY OF WIT AND WISDOM

ILLUSTRATIONS BY KATH WALKER

LESLEY MASTERS

summersdale

# Contents

Introduction ..... 7
Running Wild ..... 13
The Benefits of Gardening ..... 23
Into the Orchard ..... 31
Over the Garden Gate ..... 43
In an English Cottage Garden ..... 51
Grow Your Own ..... 56
Gardening Lore ..... 67
People in Glasshouses ..... 73
Bloomin' Lovely ..... 79
The History of Gardening ..... 93
Herb Gardens ..... 100
Tree-mendous ..... 110
When 'Hoe, Hoe, Hoe' is No Laughing Matter ..... 120
Secret Gardens and Hidden Places ..... 130
Garden Creatures Great and Small ..... 139
The Hut Parade ..... 152
Green Pastures ..... 159
Heaven on Earth ..... 165
Exotic Gardens ..... 173
A Year in the Garden ..... 181
A Gardener's Life ..... 194
Resources ..... 205

# Introduction

*No two gardens are the same.*
*No two days are the same in one garden.*

HUGH JOHNSON

A garden may be a grand park with tree-lined avenues, statuary and water features, a cottage garden filled with sweet peas and hollyhocks, a courtyard with potted plants, a simple kitchen garden or vegetable plot, a rockery, a shrubbery, an orchard, some roses round the door or even just a trug of herbs on a kitchen windowsill. Whatever the size of the garden, the benefits of gardening have been evident since man first cultivated the land. A garden is a place for calm; an escape from the hectic modern world, a place to restore mental well-being and recharge emotional batteries. You can lose yourself in gardening and allow your subconscious to wander while enjoying the sounds, smells and colours.

The physical benefits of fresh air and exercise are perhaps the most obvious: working away in the garden can be as challenging as any aerobics class, and the exertion releases endorphins which alleviate stress and lower blood pressure. Gardeners are also more likely to eat a wider variety of fruit and vegetables, and the successful harvesting of produce provides an enormous sense of achievement.

There's no denying that maintaining a garden is hard work, but even the simplest and most mundane tasks can leave you glowing with pride – it was Robert Louis Stevenson that famously said: 'I would rather do a good hour's work weeding than write two pages of my best.' All the time people are rediscovering the value of their backyards by growing their own produce and

## Introduction

seeing that home-grown is best not only for the body but the pocket, too.

Gardening and great minds go together; some of the greatest thinkers of modern times were also keen gardeners and plant lovers. This miscellany is for those who love gardens and is filled with inspiring and witty quotations, prose and poetry, as well as trivia and gardening tips and suggestions on inspirational gardens to visit.

*Grow what you love.*
*The love will keep it growing.*

EMILIE BARNES

## THE GARDENER'S FRIEND

*How so well a gardener be,*
*Here he may both hear and see*
*Every time of the year and of the moon*
*And how the crafte shall be done,*
*In what manner he shall delve and set*
*Both in drought and in wet,*
*How he shall his seeds sow;*
*Of every month he must know*
*Both of wortes and of leek,*
*Onions and of garlic,*
*Parsley, clary and eke sage*
*And all other herbage.*

*In the calendars of Januar'*
*You shall trees both set and rear*
*To grafty there on apple and pear;*
*And what trees is kind them to bear*
*Apple and a apple-tree.*
*For there is kind is most to be*
*Of pear I mind yorne*
*To graft it upon a hawthorn.*

JOHN GARDNER, 'THE FEAT OF GARDENING'

## INTRODUCTION

*The man who has planted a garden feels
that he has done something for
the good of the world.*

VITA SACKVILLE-WEST

*An addiction to gardening is not all bad when
you consider all the other choices in life.*

CORA LEA BELL

*If I'm ever reborn, I want to be a gardener –
there's too much to do for one lifetime!*

KARL FOERSTER

*Green fingers are the extension
of a verdant heart.*

RUSSELL PAGE

# Running Wild

*Gardening is civil and social,
but it wants the vigour and freedom
of the forest and the outlaw.*

HENRY DAVID THOREAU

A wild garden may seem like an oxymoron, since gardening denotes the maintenance of a planted space. Wild gardening first became popular in the early to mid nineteenth century, when the natural British landscape was considered the most romantic and idyllic of environments. William Robinson, editor of *The Garden* magazine and a renowned garden designer, introduced the concept of informal gardening to a wider audience, in stark contrast to the existing trend for formal layouts, straight paths and clipped hedging. In his book *The Wild Garden* he described using formal planting in a natural setting to create an unspoilt feel and to allow cultivated and native plants to mix. Gertrude Jekyll also championed this aesthetic. Robinson is responsible for some of today's popular garden trends, including the use of alpine plants in rock gardens and dense planting of perennials in natural-looking drifts.

*'I wouldn't want to make it look like a gardener's garden, all clipped an' spick an' span, would you?' he said. 'It's nicer like this with things runnin' wild, an' swingin' an' catchin' hold of each other.'*

FRANCES HODGSON BURNETT, *THE SECRET GARDEN*

*In garden arrangement, as in all other kinds of decorative work, one has not only to acquire a knowledge of what to do, but also to gain some wisdom in perceiving what is well to let alone.*

GERTRUDE JEKYLL

# Nature's Larder

Wild food is everywhere: blackberries on roadsides, wild garlic on riverbanks, elderberries, elderflowers and sloes in hedgerows; even dandelions are edible. It can be very satisfying to pick free, wild ingredients and make something delicious with them. And it's not just the countryside that is rich in nature's goodies – many urban paths and small gardens are mini nature reserves full of fruits, leaves and wild flowers that can be harvested. Here are a few things to look out for in your garden, along with some simple recipes to whet your appetite:

**Blackberries and mulberries** – these are the most common of the 'wild' fruits to be found in a garden. Those brambles that perhaps overhang the fence if your property backs onto wasteland or railway lines are heavy with berries in the summer, which can be made into crumbles and jams for puddings.

**Hawthorn berries** – these can be eaten raw but lack flavour when uncooked. They can be made into a jelly to add interest to a meat dish.

**Rosehips** – these bright red berries are the fruits of the rose plant. They can be used to make jams, jellies and, being rich in antioxidants and vitamin C, they make an excellent ingredient for herbal tea. In World War Two, parents were encouraged to gather up rosehips to make a vitamin-C-rich syrup for their children.

**Sloes** – these small, round blue fruits are ready to be picked after the first autumn frost. Sloe gin is a popular way of utilising these astringent berries. Here's a simple recipe:

Decant half of a litre-bottle of gin into an empty bottle and store; you will only need half the contents for this recipe. Prick or cut the sloes and place them into the bottle with the remaining gin, enough so that the liquid reaches the top. Add 150 g of sugar and screw on the top. Remember to agitate the bottle once a day to help the flavours infuse, and after two months your sloe gin will be ready to drink.

## Gardeners' Tips – make a meadow

There is no need to give up your lawn to have a meadow in your garden. By leaving a small area of your lawn unmown, you will attract all manner of plants and wildlife. Mow the patch just a handful of times a year, but look out for small creatures in the grass.

The alternative is to start with bare ground. Rake the soil to make a seedbed (poor soil is best for meadow flowers). Get an annual cornfield or wildflower mix that contains plants such as poppies, cornflowers, ox-eye daisies and cowslips, and sow in the autumn.

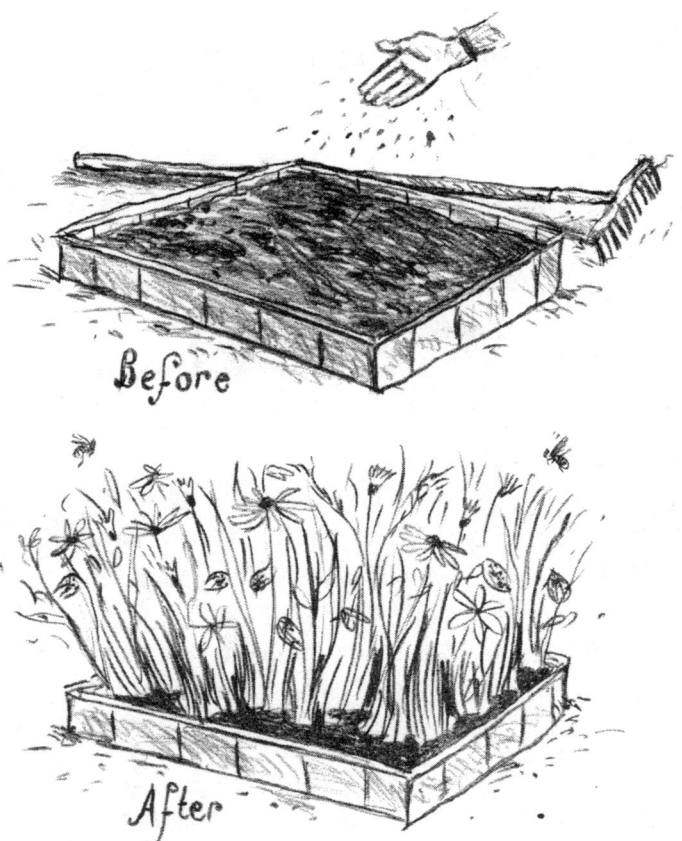

# Famous Gardener: Gertrude Jekyll

Aside from having a family name that was immortalised in Robert Louis Stevenson's novella *Dr Jekyll and Mr Hyde*, Gertrude Jekyll (1843-1932) was a major force in the Arts and Crafts Movement. She designed many gardens to complement the architecture of Edwin Lutyens, her home in Munstead Wood, near Godalming in Surrey, being a prime example. Her training as an artist inspired her to design gardens as if she were painting a canvas – using flowers as the colours in her palette and employing sensory plants, such as those with textured leaves – rather than seeing the creation of a garden as a technical exercise.

She was dedicated to creating beautiful gardens and became renowned for her huge herbaceous borders, which she would arrange from 'hot' colours to 'cold' – oranges and reds to blues and whites – and back again. She also championed traditional cottage garden plants that are still prevalent today: hostas, old-fashioned roses and lavender. She created over 400 gardens throughout her career and was also an accomplished writer, contributing more than a thousand articles to *Country Life* and *The Garden*, among other publications.

## The Gardener's Friend

*I know a bank where the wild thyme blows,*
*Where oxlips and the nodding violet grows,*
*Quite over-canopied with luscious woodbine,*
*With sweet musk-roses and with eglantine:*
*There sleeps Titania sometime of the night,*
*Lull'd in these flowers with dances and delight;*
*And there the snake throws her enamell'd skin,*
*Weed wide enough to wrap a fairy in:*
*And with the juice of this I'll streak her eyes,*
*And make her full of hateful fantasies.*
*Take thou some of it, and seek through this grove:*
*A sweet Athenian lady is in love*
*With a disdainful youth: anoint his eyes;*
*But do it when the next thing he espies*
*May be the lady: thou shalt know the man*
*By the Athenian garments he hath on.*
*Effect it with some care, that he may prove*
*More fond on her than she upon her love:*
*And look thou meet me ere the first cock crow.*

William Shakespeare, Oberon's speech in *A Midsummer Night's Dream*

# The Benefits of Gardening

*All my hurts my garden spade can heal.*

RALPH WALDO EMERSON

## The Gardener's Friend

Regular tasks that are essential for maintaining a garden – such as weeding, composting, mowing and raking leaves – keep you fit and give you the added advantage of being in the open air and not some featureless gym. Here is a guide to the calories that can be burned when you're working away in the garden:

- Weeding (digging out the roots, rather than spraying herbicides!) burns around 330 calories per hour. This works your upper- and lower-body muscles.
- Mowing the lawn or pushing a wheelbarrow for an hour will burn 300 calories.
- Digging and shovelling is great for building upper-body strength and burns about 250 calories an hour.
- Watering the plants with a watering can will burn around 150 calories, and the simple act of picking flowers will burn about the same amount.
- And after all that physical exertion and fresh air you're far less likely to have trouble sleeping.

## The Benefits of Gardening

*Gardening and laughing are two of the best things in life you can do to promote good health and a sense of well-being.*

David Hobson

*My garden of flowers is also my garden of thoughts and dreams. The thoughts grow as freely as the flowers, and the dreams are as beautiful.*

Abram L. Urban

P rince Charles famously said, 'I happily talk to the plants and trees, and listen to them. I think it's absolutely crucial.' He was ridiculed for this at the time, but he maintained that it kept him sane and that it was also beneficial to the health of his plants. This theory has since been tested by the Royal Horticultural Society's Wisley Gardens in Surrey, where recordings of Shakespeare's works and John Wyndham's *The Day of the Triffids* have been played to ten tomato plants around the clock. The voice recordings were channelled to the roots with compact headphones.

The findings suggest that low-frequency sounds elicit the most favourable response, as they vibrate the plant and encourage growth. So a deep Barry White drawl is the voice that you should aim for! Incidentally, *The Day of the Triffids*, a nightmarish vision of man-eating plants, might seem an odd choice, but the experts claim that, to a tomato plant, the story of the arrival of triffids into neglected gardens would be nothing short of inspirational.

A similar trial was carried out by Dorothy Retallack in 1973. She published her findings in her book *The Sound of Music and Plants*. Her findings showed that easy-listening music encouraged growth whereas rock music 'damaged' the plants and increased their water consumption needs.

## The Benefits of Gardening

*The garden is a ground
plot for the mind.*

Thomas Hill

'O Tiger-lily,' said Alice, addressing herself to one that was waving gracefully about in the wind, 'I wish you could talk!'
'We can talk,' said the Tiger-lily, 'when there's anybody worth talking to.'

Alice was so astonished that she couldn't speak for a minute: it quite seemed to take her breath away. At length, as the Tiger-lily only went on waving about, she spoke again, in a timid voice – almost a whisper. 'And can all the flowers talk?'

'As well as you can,' said the Tiger-lily. 'And a great deal louder.'

'It isn't manners for us to begin, you know,' said the Rose, 'and I really was wondering when you'd speak! Said I to myself, "Her face has got some sense in it, though it's not a clever one!" Still you're the right colour, and that goes a long way.'

'I don't care about the colour,' the Tiger-lily remarked. 'If only her petals curled up a little more, she'd be all right.'

> Lewis Carroll, *Through the Looking-Glass,
> and What Alice Found There*

## The Benefits of Gardening

*A garden is a grand teacher. It teaches patience and careful watchfulness; it teaches industry and thrift; above all it teaches entire trust.*

GERTRUDE JEKYLL

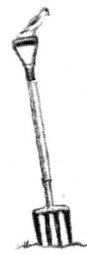

*The many great gardens of the world, of literature and poetry, of painting and music, of religion and architecture, all make the point as clear as possible: the soul cannot thrive in the absence of a garden.*

THOMAS MORE

*As I work among my flowers, I find myself talking to them, reasoning and remonstrating with them, and adoring them as if they were human beings. Much laughter I provoke among my friends by so doing, but that is of no consequence. We are on such good terms, my flowers and I!*

CELIA THAXTER, *AN ISLAND GARDEN*

# Into the Orchard

*In an orchard there should be enough to eat, enough to lay up, enough to be stolen, and enough to rot on the ground.*

James Boswell

# Quinces

The quince is believed to be the antecedent of apples and pears – and looks very much like a yellow-skinned pear when ripe, with a sweet, delicate scent. It is rarely seen on the supermarket shelves, but quince trees are a common and often-overlooked plant in British gardens. You can't eat the fruit raw but the flesh can be cooked and made into delicious pastes and jellies, or you can make a simple dessert of baked quince by cooking it in the same way as a baked apple. It was a popular fruit in medieval times, and it is famously eaten in Edward Lear's 'Owl and the Pussycat':

*They dined on mince, and slices of quince,*
*Which they ate with a runcible spoon;*
*And hand in hand, on the edge of the sand,*
*They danced by the light of the moon...'*

## Medlars

This unusual fruit was once popular in Victorian times, but because it requires 'bletting' (softening, either through storage or by frost) in order to become edible, it has faded into obscurity in recent times. It looks to the untrained eye like a spoilt apple, with its base resembling a twisted star or something that has been nibbled at by a voracious band of hornets. Because the fruit is effectively rotten before it's regarded as ripe, the unfortunate medlar has been used figuratively in literature as a symbol for prostitution – in Shakespeare's *Measure For Measure*, for example, Lucio denies his past dalliances because 'they would else have married me to the rotten medlar'. Despite its unsavoury literary past, once bletted the flesh of the medlar has the flavour and consistency of apple sauce, which tastes delicious as an accompaniment to cheese.

# Figs

The fig has been a symbol of fertility since biblical times. In some Mediterranean countries the sap is used to anoint women who are trying to conceive. It is one of the most ancient of the cultivated fruit trees, and it needs a sheltered position to thrive and plenty of space for its sprawling roots, so if you're consider having one in your garden don't plant it near the house. The fruits grow one year and ripen in the second year. Seeds are produced when female fig wasps force their way inside the young fruits to lay their eggs. These eggs hatch into larvae which mate, after which the impregnated females push their way out of the fruit covered in pollen and visit another plant to repeat the process. Fig trees are quite hardy and can grow happily as far north as Scotland, provided they have a bit of shelter, preferably against a south-facing wall.

## Plums

Confucius wrote about plums as early as 479 BC, and Pompey the Great introduced them to Roman orchards in 65 BC. Surprisingly, they are the second most cultivated fruit in the world, next to apples. They are the simplest stone fruit to grow in the UK, the common varieties being: Victoria, Cambridge Gage, Warwickshire Drooper, Merryweather Damson and Opal.

*Our homestead flowers and fruited trees*
*May Eden's orchard shame;*
*We taste the tempting sweets of these*
*Like Eve, without her blame.*

JOHN GREENLEAF WHITTIER, FROM 'GARDEN'

*If love were a tree, then feelings would be the fruit. A good tree brings forth good fruit in season.*

JOSEPH CUBBY

## PEARS

Records show that pears were cultivated in gardens over 4,000 years ago. Homer described this sweet fruit in *The Odyssey* as 'a gift from the gods', and in *Naturalis Historia*, an encyclopedia published in AD 77–79, Pliny the Elder recommended stewing them with honey. Cooked pears were traditionally eaten as an accompaniment to meats until the sixteenth century, rather than in their raw state. Popular varieties include conference, winter nellis, Louise Bonne de Jersey and Doyenné du Comice.

# Apples

This most popular of orchard fruits has been depicted as the 'forbidden fruit' in the story of the Garden of Eden and as a poisoned gift in the fairy tale of Snow White. One old wives' tale claims that if a young girl were to peel the skin of an apple in one continuous thread and then throw the peeling over her left shoulder, the peel would make the initial of her true love. A recent study showed that the apple contains more genes than humans, over 57,000.

## Popular apple varieties

There are over 1,200 varieties of native British apple and many have wonderful names. Here are just a few of them:

Allington Pippin, Annie Elizabeth, Barnack Beauty, Beeley Pippin, Bismarck, Bundy's Ringwood Red, Bushy Grove, Catshead, Chivers Delight, D'Arcy Spice, Falstaff, Fearn's Pippin, Laxton's Fortune, Greensleeves, Hoary Morning, Keswick Codlin, Merton Knave, Morgan Sweet, Newton Wonder, Winston, Winter Banana.

# Gardeners' Tips – storing fruit

If you would prefer to store your fruit harvest, you have a number of options:

**Strawberries, raspberries, currants and hedgerow fruits** – open-freeze these as soon as they are picked by laying them on trays and placing them in the freezer. Once completely frozen, decant them into plastic bags and seal them.

**Pears and apples** – wrap these individually in newspaper and store them in wooden boxes or drawers, and keep cool. An unheated garage or shed would be ideal. Keep an eye on the wrapped fruits and check regularly for fruit that has gone off.

**All fruits** – drying fruit is a great way of making your harvest last. Use only blemish-free ripe fruits. Wash, pit and slice the fruits to a uniform size. Blanch the pieces by steaming them in a steamer or colander suspended above a pan of boiling water for five minutes and then plunge the pieces into cold water – this preserves their colour. Dip the pieces in a mixture of water and a few squeezes of fresh lemon juice – this helps to reduce browning. Then leave the pieces to dry on kitchen paper. Once dry, place on parchment-covered baking trays and put them in the oven on a low heat, about 120°C, for four hours, but keep checking on the fruit to see if it's cooked. It should be chewy when it's ready to eat. Let the pieces stand overnight before storing them in airtight containers, and then freeze them to eliminate any germs that may be present. Defrost the pieces, then enjoy!

*And still she slept an azure-lidded sleep,*
*In blanched linen, smooth and lavender'd,*
*While he forth from the closet brought a heap*
*Of candied apples, quince, and plum, and gourd;*
*With jellies, soother than the creamy curd,*
*And lucent syrops, tinct with cinnamon;*
*Manna and dates, In argosy transferr'd*
*From Fez; and spiced dainties, everyone,*
*From silken Samarcand to cedar'd Lebanon.*

JOHN KEATS, FROM 'THE EVE OF ST AGNES'

# Make Your Own Cider

If you have a glut of apples, try making cider. Choose a mixture of sweet and sharp apple varieties (try sweet: Pink Lady and Golden Pippin, and sharp: Cox's Pomona and Brown's Apple). Use ripe ones from the tree mixed with windfall apples, leaving them to stand for a few days to soften. You will need a scratter to roughly pulp the apples.

You will then need an apple press. Pour some of the pulp over a piece of muslin that's been laid within the frame of the apple press. Fold the rest of the muslin over the mixture and add another layer of the mixture to the next layer, and so on, until you have built up enough layers to reach the top of the apple press. Then begin to press the layers to extract the apple juice, which will collect in the container below the press. Leave the juice to ferment for several months – add yeast and sugar at your discretion; many cider makers choose to let the juice ferment naturally. While the juice is fermenting, you will need to clear away the pips and stalks and any other detritus from the liquid. When it is ready, decant the cider into sterilised bottles or a large keg, then drink!

You can make perry – using pears instead of apples – in the same way.

## Into the Orchard

*Taste every fruit of every tree in
the garden at least once.*

STEPHEN FRY

*A man is old when he can pass an apple
orchard and not remember the stomach ache.*

JAMES RUSSELL LOWELL

## Gardeners' Tips – growing fruit trees in small outside spaces

Even if your garden extends to little more than a narrow balcony, you can still successfully grow fruit trees in containers – dwarf trees are ideally suited to this and a sunny south-facing spot is best.

Choose wood or plastic containers rather than terracotta pots, because while terracotta may look more attractive the plants inside them tend to dry out quicker. A large pot is preferable – about 50 cm in diameter – to ensure that the tree doesn't become pot-bound.

Choose from dwarf varieties of citrus trees, including lemons, limes and oranges, as well as orchard fruits such as apples, pears and cherries. Container trees don't reach the height of those planted in the ground, but the fruit they produce will be of normal size and just as delicious.

# Over the Garden Gate

*Placemaking, and a good English garden depend entirely on principle and have very little to do with fashion.*

LANCELOT 'CAPABILITY' BROWN

# Ten Famous British Gardens to Visit

**Sissinghurst Castle Garden, Kent** – in this romantic garden you will encounter rare plants mingling with the traditional as you weave your way through the intimate garden 'rooms'. This is the home of plantswoman Sarah Raven and was once the residence of writer Vita Sackville-West, who created the garden.

**Nyman's Garden, West Sussex** – transforming itself across the seasons, this garden benefits not only from a rare collection of plants sourced from around the world, it also holds a spectacular position at the top of the South Downs.

**The Lost Gardens of Heligan, Cornwall** – after many years of neglect the gardens have been revived to their former glory and now boast a famous collection of camellias and rhododendrons, as well as the 'jungle'.

**Inverewe Gardens, Ross-shire** – despite its latitude, this garden takes advantage of the nearby Gulf Stream to create a tropical paradise, home to over 5,000 exotic species.

Sissinghurst Castle Garden

**Chatsworth House, Derbyshire** – developed over six centuries, the garden is set within a magical landscape that abounds with rare species and natural walkways. The Salisbury Lawns, created by Capability Brown in the eighteenth century, are home to the renowned 300-year-old cascade water feature.

**Powis Castle, Powys** – within the grounds of this spectacular medieval fortress is its world-famous terraced garden, which dates from the 1670s. Another feature of note is its enormous clipped yews.

**Tresco Gardens, Isles of Scilly** – self-styled as a 'perennial Kew without the glass', this tropical garden in the Atlantic Ocean contains 20,000 exotic plants from over 80 countries, interspersed with mastheads from ships that have been wrecked off the coast.

**Great Dixter, Northiam, nr Rye, East Sussex** – the grounds of this Lutyens-designed house are the life's work of the owner Christopher Lloyd and his head gardener Fergus Garrett. It incorporates yew topiary, meadows, the famous Long Border and an exotic garden.

**Hampton Court Palace, Surrey** – in its 750 acres on the banks of the Thames is the world-famous box yew maze, a recreation of the Privy Garden designed for William III with original planting and marble sculptures, a fountain garden and a deer park.

**Mount Stewart House, Co. Down, Northern Ireland** – this National Trust garden, constructed in the 1920s by Edith Vane-Tempest-Stewart, Lady Londonderry, benefits from the unique microclimate of the Ards Peninsula. It is renowned for its fountains, multi-sensory activity trails and 'Temple of the Winds'.

*Should it not be remembered that in setting a garden we are painting a picture?*

BEATRIX JONES FARRAND

# Famous Gardener: Vita Sackville-West

Vita Sackville-West (1892–1962) was a renowned novelist and poet, and a key figure in the Bloomsbury group of writers and artists. Her passion for gardening began in 1913 after her marriage to Harold Nicolson, a diplomat and biographer, at which point she started to experiment through trial and error in the gardens at their first home, Long Barn in Kent. By the time they moved to the Elizabethan ruin of Sissinghurst Castle in 1930, the couple had developed a complementary gardening dynamic where Nicolson would be responsible for the architectural layout – paths, walls, formal hedging and the like – and Sackville-West would focus on planting. Her principle was to let self-seeded and cultivated plants mingle, but to adhere to a strict seasonal cycle and colour palette. They landscaped the extensive gardens from scratch, creating intimate 'rooms' which showcased the classical sensibilities of Nicolson and the romantic, abundant planting of Sackville-West. One of her finest achievements at Sissinghurst is the one-colour gardens, such as the White Garden, which is still a feature today – it is full of white, grey and silver plants that are transformed by a moonlit night, when the flowers and shrubs look almost luminescent.

It was Sackville-West's passion for gardening rather than any formal expertise that led her to be commissioned to write a regular column for *The Observer* newspaper from 1946, which was so well received that journalist and author Anne Scott-James claimed her articles had done 'more to change the face of English gardening than any other writing since Robinson's *The English Flower Garden*.' She also became a founding member of the National Trust's garden committee in 1948, and her beloved Sissinghurst Castle gardens were transferred to the Trust in 1967.

*The kiss of the sun for pardon,*
*The song of the birds for mirth,*
*One is nearer to God's heart in a garden*
*Than anywhere else on earth.*

DOROTHY FRANCES GURNEY, 'GARDEN THOUGHTS'

# IN AN ENGLISH COTTAGE GARDEN

*The garden is never dead; growth is always going on, and growth that can be seen, and seen with delight.*

Henry Ellacombe, *In My Vicarage Garden*

*The house, granary, wall and paling, are covering with vines, cherry trees, roses, honeysuckles, and jessamines, with great clusters of tall hollyhocks running up between them; a large elder overhanging the little gate, and a magnificent bay-tree...*

Mary Russell Mitford describing her cottage garden in 1832

## Gardeners' Tips – how to get the best out of your blooms

**Roses** – to get the best display from your rose bushes, bury banana skins just below the surface of the soil surrounding them. The skins will rot quickly, releasing calcium, magnesium, potassium and other beneficial nutrients.

**Foxgloves** – these flowers are not only striking; they also stimulate the growth of other plants and help fend off diseases. Traditionally a hedgerow plant, these strikingly beautiful sentinels were popularised by Gertrude Jekyll in her white planting schemes and are now a common feature in British gardens.

**Sunflowers** – these will thrive if planted around your compost heap, and when they grow tall they'll make it look less unsightly. Just make sure you leave an opening to access the compost without damaging the flowers.

*Ah! Sun-flower! Weary of time,*
*Who countest the steps of the Sun:*
*Seeking after that sweet golden clime,*
*Where the traveller's journey is done.*

WILLIAM BLAKE, FROM 'AH! SUNFLOWER!'

*I used to visit and revisit it a dozen times a day, and stand in deep contemplation over my vegetable progeny with a love that nobody could share or conceive of who had never taken part in the process of creation.*

NATHANIEL HAWTHORNE, *MOSSES FROM AN OLD MANSE*

## In an English Cottage Garden

*In the garden snowdrops, crocuses, hyacinths, magnolias, roses, lilies, asters, the dahlia in all its varieties, pear trees and apple trees and cherry trees and mulberry trees evergreen and perennial, grew so thick on each other's roots that there was no plot of earth without its bloom, and no stretch of sward without its shade.*

VIRGINIA WOOLF, *ORLANDO*

# Grow Your Own

*In order to live off a garden,
you practically have to live in it.*

FRANK MCKINNEY HUBBARD

## Grow Your Own

*Earth is here so kind, that just tickle her with a hoe and she laughs with a harvest.*

Douglas William Jerrold

*If well managed, nothing is more beautiful than the kitchen garden: the earliest blooms come there: we shall in vain seek for flowering shrubs... equal to peaches, nectarines, apricots, and plums.*

William Cobbett, *The English Gardener*

# Carrots

The wild carrot is native to South West Asia, Afghanistan and Europe, and seeds have been found from the Mesolithic period around 10,000 years ago. It was the seeds that were first used, rather than the roots, and there are records dating from the sixteenth century of herbalists using them to treat those who suffered from stomach ailments or bites from venomous creatures. Over the centuries the humble carrot went from being a spindly, bitter-tasting woody root to a sweet-tasting, crunchy vegetable.

They come in a surprising variety of colours – yellow, white, purple, red and orange. The familiar orange carrot was first grown in the Netherlands in the seventeenth century and soon became popular, especially with followers of the Dutch House of Orange. Planting carrots with your tomatoes will increase your tomato harvest, and if you allow the carrots to flower, they will attract wasps that will destroy many garden pests.

## Potatoes

This most versatile of vegetables was first cultivated in the Andes in South America, being a hardy plant that can grow in poor soil and fluctuating temperatures. The Spanish Conquistadors came across the potato in the mid sixteenth century, when they were plundering Peru and its surrounding gold-rich countries, and brought it to Europe, where it was grown by botanists primarily for curiosity as it was recognised as a member of the poisonous nightshade family and unlikely to appeal to the civilised palate.

History suggests Sir Francis Drake introduced the potato to British shores in the late sixteenth century, when, after battling the Spaniards in the Caribbean, he stopped at the Colombian port of Cartagena to gather provisions – including tobacco and potato tubers.

This vegetable contains most of the vitamins needed for sustenance and became the staple diet of the poor, but of course by the 1840s the failed crops in Ireland caused by potato blight fungus resulted in famine. A fungicide was eventually developed in 1883, and now the humble potato is a firm favourite.

## Onions

Onions were cultivated in China over 5,000 years ago. They are also described in the ancient Vedic writings from India and have been traced back to 3500 BC in Egypt. Egyptologists discovered onions in the eye sockets of the entombed King Ramses IV, who died in 1160 BC. It was believed that the strong, eye-watering scent of the onions would prompt the dead to breathe again, and that the onion's medicinal properties would also have been beneficial in the afterlife.

The Ancient Greeks also held onions in high regard; the original Olympic athletes would eat copious quantities of the vegetable, drink the juice and go as far as rubbing onion skins over their bodies before competing, believing that it would lighten the balance of their blood and firm their muscles. Onions were a diet staple for both rich and poor by the Middle Ages. Such is their value, they were once used as rent payments and wedding gifts. They have antioxidant properties, which can help to block cancer, and they appear to lower cholesterol.

*Does Madame want melons as well?* asks Hilaire with seeming irrelevance. *Of course she does! What sane woman would not want the miracle of melons growing daily in the open air of her garden? Then the melons must be planted at least one hectare away from the courgettes so that they cannot see each other,* affirms Hilaire.

'*Si non, ils se marient*' *explains Hilaire to a mystified Madame, and the melons will become courgettes. Why do not courgettes become melons? laments Madame. But it appears that in Nature with mixed alliances the plebeian type usually triumphs.*

LADY FORTESCUE, *PERFUME FROM PROVENCE*

# Gardeners' Tips – storing your root vegetables

Get some wooden boxes, or an old set of drawers, and spread a layer of sand at the bottom of each one. Place a selection of vegetables on the sand, cover them with more sand, then add another layer of vegetables. Keep doing this until you reach the top of the box, making sure that all vegetables are covered. Label and date the boxes/drawers and store in an unheated but dry place, such as an outhouse or shed. Potatoes can be scrubbed and put in old hessian sacks. Store in a cool, dry place and check them occasionally for rot or slug damage.

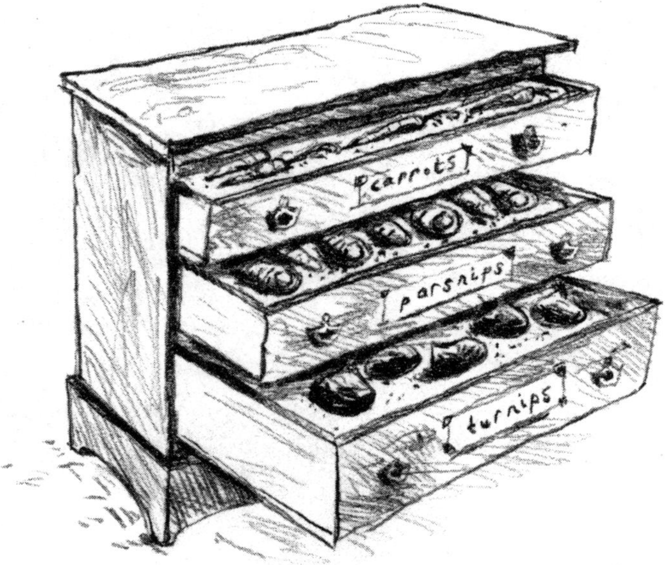
carrots
parsnips
turnips

*He had been eight years upon a project for extracting sunbeams out of cucumbers, which were to be put into vials hermetically sealed, and let out to warm the air in raw, inclement summers.*

JONATHAN SWIFT, *GULLIVER'S TRAVELS*

*Cauliflower is nothing but cabbage with a college education.*

MARK TWAIN

## Gardeners' Tips – how to deal with gluts

Once you've made enough 'glutney' (chutney made out of whatever is in glut in your garden) or 'jampote' (jam and compotes), there are other ways, apart from storing, to put your excess harvest to good use:

- ❀ Offer your fresh vegetables to a hospice, refuge or charitable organisation.

- ❀ Get involved with SwapCrop, www.swapcrop.co.uk, which encourages local communities across the UK to swap their excess crops, as well as sharing recipes and growing tips.

- ❀ Add them to your compost heap (but only if they are pest-free and have not been treated with herbicides during the growing process) and create your own organic soil for growing next year's crops.

*I'd planted an immense number of things I would never get around to eating because I hadn't expected all of them to come up. OH [Other Half] reckoned that when he was a boy, half the seeds he'd planted had failed to come up and half the ones that came up had been eaten by slugs, so we'd sown our crops on that basis. Everything, but everything, had come up: I'd been giving away cucumbers for three weeks, and neighbours were starting to pretend they weren't home when I knocked on their doors. I was sometimes tempted to post cucumbers through letterboxes, but so far I'd restrained myself.*

KAY SEXTON, *MINDING MY PEAS AND CUCUMBERS: QUIRKY TALES OF ALLOTMENT LIFE*

# Gardening Lore

*She could grow them [flowers] anywhere... and they seemed to live longer for her.*

LAURIE LEE, *CIDER WITH ROSIE*

# Gardening By the Moon

This isn't something only practised by vampires or night owls, it's an ancient gardening tradition that involves being guided by the phases of the moon. Some swear by it for healthier plants and higher crop yields. Start by making a note of the new and full moons; this will determine when the moon is waxing and waning.

**Waxing moon**
This is the time of growth, so it's the best moment to sow seeds and do planting, as well as prune existing plants to encourage new shoots and healthy growth.

**Waning moon**
This quieter period in the garden signifies reduced growth, so mow the lawn and clear away the weeds.

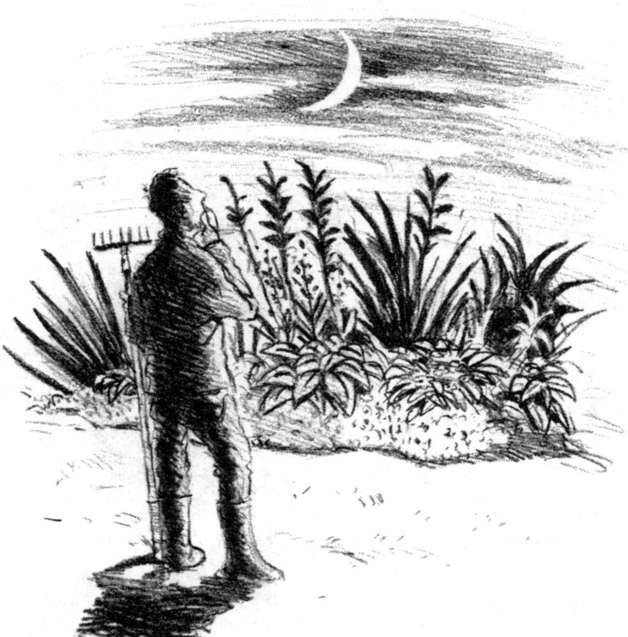

*Neither graft, set, sow, nor plant
anything that day whereon there
happeneth an Eclipse either of Sun
or Moon, or when the Moon is
afflicted by the infortunes
Saturn or Mars.*

REVEREND SAMUEL GILBERT, *THE FLORIST'S VADE-MECUM*

*Gardening is the art that uses flowers and plants as paint, and the soil and sky as canvas.*

ELIZABETH MURRAY

## OLD WIVES' TALES FOR GARDENERS

When planting peas, fill the trench with holly leaves to protect the pea shoots from mice. It is considered lucky if the first pea pod that you shell has a single pea inside.

Taking hawthorn into the house is believed to be very unlucky, as it brings with it a year of ill health.

Sweeping the house with a broom made of birch twigs will rid the place of witches.

*Nature does not complete things. She is chaotic.
Man must finish, and he does so by making
a garden and building a wall.*

ROBERT FROST

*They called him the 'garden sorcerer'... The old
man had seen half the world's gardens, but
preferred the dark corners of small courtyards
or balconies where a few straggling
geraniums might be growing.*

GIOVANNI ARPINO, *IL MAGO DEI GIARDINI*

# People in Glasshouses

*Who loves a garden loves a greenhouse too,*
*Unconscious of a less propitious clime,*
*There bloom exotic beauty, warm and snug,*
*While the winds whistle, and the snows descend.*

WILLIAM COWPER, *THE TASK*

# No Pane, No Gain!

One of the earliest precursors to the modern-day greenhouse was a specularium constructed in AD 30 for Emperor Tiberius out of tiny translucent sheets of mica. Its primary use was growing cucumbers after Tiberius was taken ill and his physicians instructed him to eat one of these fruits a day.

It was not until the thirteenth century that Bavarian Albertus Magnus, a Dominican friar and incidentally one of the great scholars of the time, wrote on the subject of the Roman practice of forcing plants in hothouses. His experiments in 'hothousing' were so successful that he was accused of witchcraft, and he narrowly avoided execution.

Early slate-roofed greenhouses were in use from the seventeenth century, but they were very high maintenance because gardeners were expected to walk around the perimeter of these 'hot' houses with fire baskets containing glowing coals to keep the crops warm!

Before the widespread introduction of glasshouses, the gardeners of the eighteenth century used 'hotbeds' in order to grow plants from warmer climates, and to make the ground they worked productive in the winter months. The hotbed relied on the heat generated from decomposing manure, which made it rather smelly and necessitated its separation and screening off from the rest of the garden. Philip Miller in his *Gardener's Dictionary* published in 1731 described how he would harvest asparagus in January and traditional summer salad vegetables in February.

Wardian cases, which are rather like miniature greenhouses, were used in the mid nineteenth century to protect and propagate non-native plants. A Wardian case was used by Robert Fortune in 1848 to transport seedlings of tea plants from China to India, thus establishing India's tea industry.

# Famous Gardener: Sir Joseph Paxton

According to his obituary in *The Times*, Sir Joseph Paxton (1803–65) was 'the greatest gardener of his time, the founder of a new style of architecture, and a man of genius'. He combined skills in engineering, horticulture and artistry not only landscape the grounds at Chatsworth House in Derbyshire in his capacity as head gardener there, but also to design the original Crystal Palace that was used to house The Great Exhibition of 1851. This great spectacle stimulated huge public interest in glasshouses, and many people wanted small glass structures and conservatories in their own gardens. In response to this demand, Paxton launched a successful range of affordable flat-pack conservatories and greenhouses with the catchy slogan 'Hothouses for the Million'.

He was one of nine children, and the son of a farm labourer who died when Joseph was seven. He began his career at 13 as an apprentice gardener at Battlesdon Park in Bedfordshire, where he received his grounding in kitchen gardening. He later moved to Woodhall, Suffolk, and then back to Battlesdon before joining the Horticultural Society's Garden in Chiswick as a labourer. It was here, at the age of 23, that he met William George Spencer Cavendish, the sixth Duke of Devonshire, who, impressed by Paxton's natural gardening talent and politeness, offered him the position of head gardener at his home, Chatsworth House.

In an account of his first day at Chatsworth he describes arriving at the grounds at 4.30 in the morning, scaling the gate to look around, then setting his new team to work by six o'clock, watching the water works in action and then having breakfast with one Mrs Gregory and her niece, 'the latter fell in love with me and I with her, and thus completed my first morning's work at Chatsworth before nine o'clock.' The staggering ornamental gardens at Chatsworth are testament to his belief that art and nature, and the informal and formal, could happily coexist.

## The Gardener's Friend

*The herbaceous smell in an English greenhouse reminds me of my grandmother Iris, who was an exceptional gardener.*

ROSE GRAY

*For myself I hold no preferences among flowers, so long as they are wild, free, spontaneous. Bricks to all greenhouses. Blackthumb and cutworm to the potted plant.*

EDWARD ABBEY

# Bloomin' Lovely

*People from a planet without flowers would think we must be mad with joy the whole time to have such things about us.*

Iris Murdoch

*It is a greater act of faith to plant
a bulb than to plant a tree.*

CLARE LEIGHTON, *FOUR HEDGES*

*There is material enough in a single flower for
the ornament of a score of cathedrals.*

JOHN RUSKIN

# Roses

The first roses grew around 35 million years ago, and today there are an astonishing 35,000 varieties. Wild roses were used in the production of rosewater as far back as 2000 BC, and there is evidence that roses were widely cultivated in China in 500 BC and by the Romans and other early European civilisations. In fact, roses became synonymous with the worst excesses of the Roman Empire, when the poorest were forced to grow roses in place of edible crops to satisfy their rulers. These rulers would bathe in rose-scented water and conduct their feasts on carpets of rose petals.

It wasn't until the late eighteenth century that cultivated roses were introduced into Britain from China. Most modern-day roses can be traced back to this time. Roses are not just beautiful to look at and smell – their petals can be used to make a delicate-flavoured jelly or syrup, and the edible fruits, known as rosehips, are used for making tea and jams.

*I don't know whether nice people tend to grow roses or growing roses makes people nice.*

ROLAND A. BROWNE

*It will never rain roses. When we want to have more roses, we must plant more roses.*

GEORGE ELIOT

## Daffodils, or Narcissi

Narcissus was a beautiful youth of classical Greek legend who became so entranced with his own reflection that he pined away and the gods turned him into a flower: the humble daffodil. Although, strictly speaking, the name daffodil applies only to the larger trumpet-like flowers (the short-cupped and multi-headed blooms are known as narcissi), many gardeners refer to all kinds as daffodils.

As early as about 300 BC, the Greek botanist and philosopher Theophrastus listed and described many of the earliest known kinds of narcissus in his nine-volume *Enquiry into Plants*. However, it was not until the nineteenth century that classification of the many narcissus species was attempted.

They are a sign that spring has sprung, and that warm, sunny days are round the corner, but there are also winter varieties. The perianths (petals) are mostly yellow or white but can occasionally be orange, green, red or a combination of these colours. Today, many cultivars have brightly coloured coronas (cups), which may be yellow, white, pink, orange, red, green or a mixture of these.

*Consider the lilies of the field, how they grow: they toil not, neither do they spin: even Solomon in all his glory was not arrayed like one of these.*

MATTHEW 6:28-29

# Lilies

Lilies are the stuff of legend; in Roman mythology the story goes that when Venus rose from the sea she saw a lily and was consumed with jealousy at its whiteness and beauty, so she caused a large pistil to spring from its centre. Yet it remains a symbol of purity and virtue, being a popular bridal flower as well as a symbol of condolence. In Victorian times, British plant explorers searched the globe for new plants and found many species of lily including the orange *Lilium henryi*, or Henry's lily, which is named after botanist Augustine Henry. Another famous plant explorer was an Englishman named E. H. Wilson, who found so many plants in China that he earned the nickname 'Chinese Wilson'. One of his most notable discoveries was the white *Lilium regale*, the regal lily. Though they will make an exquisite addition to your flower patch, be aware that they are poisonous to cats.

# Tulips

The word 'tulip' derives from the Turkish word for 'turban', and it was the Turks that first cultivated this flower in AD 1000. Before that it was growing as a wild flower in Central Asia. Carolus Clusius, a sixteenth-century Dutch botanist and pharmacist, received a collection of tulip bulbs and seeds from the Austrian ambassador to the Ottoman Empire, and introduced the flower to the Netherlands.

By the beginning of the seventeenth century, the tulip was being grown in gardens in Western Europe because of its bright colours and frilly petals. It soon became very sought-after, particularly in the Netherlands, where the bulbs were sold for vast sums, the hybrids being the highest status symbols of the day. 'Tulipmania' reached its zenith in late 1636, where some of the rarest varieties achieved higher prices than houses. The craze permeated all classes of Dutch society as homes, estates and industries were mortgaged to purchase bulbs that could then be sold for higher prices.

Eventually, of course, values could climb no higher and the market collapsed, leaving tulip traders and speculators bankrupt overnight. The crash did little to mar the tulip's reputation, however, and it continues to be a vital part of the Dutch flower industry and the national flower of Holland.

A half-moon, dusky gold, was sinking behind the black sycamore at the end of the garden, making the sky dull purple with its glow. Nearer, a dim white fence of lilies went across the garden, and the air all round them seemed to stir with scent... He went across the beds of pinks, whose keen perfume came sharply across the rocking, heavy scent of the lilies, and stood alongside the white barrier of flowers. They flagged all loose, as if they were panting. The scent made him drunk.

      D. H. LAWRENCE, *SONS AND LOVERS*

# Hollyhocks

The rather jolly hollyhock, a member of the mallow family, is a favourite of the quintessential English country garden. These popular flowers were first cultivated in Sicily in the seventeenth century at a botanical garden near Palermo. Prior to this, they were believed to have grown wild in South America and China. They are easy to grow, even flourishing in poor soil and full sun, next to fences and hedges and through cracks in patios. They can grow to eight feet, and they come in an amazing array of pinks, purples, yellows, reds and whites. An infusion of dried hollyhock flower heads is a traditional remedy for coughs and mouth ulcers.

## Sweet peas

These delicate and beautifully scented climbing flowers originate from Italy. They come in a range of pretty pinks, purples, whites and reds. They appear in John Keats' poem 'I Stood Tip-Toe Upon a Little Hill':

*'Here are sweet peas, on tip-toe for a flight:*
*With wings of gentle flush o'er delicate white,*
*And taper fingers catching at all things,*
*To bind them all about with tiny rings.'*

# Edible Flowers

Flowers can be used for all sorts of culinary purposes. Here are some ideas for inspiration in the kitchen:

**Courgette flowers** – these can be deep-fried in batter or stuffed with cheese and herbs and gently fried for an accompaniment to pasta.

**Nasturtiums and pansies** – these vibrant-looking flowers make a peppery addition to a salad.

**Violets** – dipped in egg white and dusted with icing sugar, these delicate flowers make pretty cake decorations.

**Elderflowers** – collect these flowers that often grow in wild gardens and hedgerows, and make a cordial or use the flower heads to make fritters.

To make the fritters you will need an egg, 50 g of flour, 100 ml of milk and five large elderflower heads. First, mix the egg yolk, flour and milk together to make a basic batter. Leave to stand for half an hour and then fold in the whisked egg white. Heat oil in a pan or fryer. Dip the elderflower heads in the batter and fry them for a couple of minutes, then place on kitchen paper to drain the excess oil before eating.

*The actual flower is the plant's highest fulfilment, and are not here exclusively for herbaria, county floras and plant geography: they are here first of all for delight.*

JOHN RUSKIN

*It is a golden maxim to cultivate the garden for the nose, and the eyes will take care of themselves.*

ROBERT LOUIS STEVENSON

# The History of Gardening

*God almighty first planted a garden. And indeed, it is the purest of human pleasures.*

Francis Bacon

*Let us divide our labours, thou where choice
Leads thee, or where most needs, whether to wind
The Woodbine round this Arbour, or direct
The clasping Ivie where to climb, while I
In yonder Spring of Roses intermixt
With Myrtle, find what to redress till Noon.*

JOHN MILTON, FROM *PARADISE LOST*

# A Potted History of Gardening

**First century AD:** the earliest known ornamental garden in Britain was cultivated by the Romans in Fishbourne, West Sussex. The gardens were set out in a formal geometric design of low-level box-hedging, which lined long walkways. These paths led to small niches that would contain sculptures or water features. There was also a kitchen garden containing herbs, vegetables and fruits, including grapevines, an expanse of lawn and climbing roses on wooden trellises.

**1066:** the Normans introduced a spate of new plants to British shores, such as lavender and borage.

**1200:** crops were essential to the self-sufficiency of monasteries at this time. As well as vegetable crops, the practice of kitchen gardening was developed to provide plants for cooking and medicinal remedies. Castles also contained kitchen gardens.

**1256–1277:** the first English gardener was named in the royal accounts of Henry III as Edmund the Gardener. He received two and a half pence a day for his gardening services at Windsor Castle.

**1530:** plant species began to be exchanged between Europe and the Americas.

**1568**: Thomas Hill published the first book of general gardening skills entitled *The Profitable Arte of Gardening*. It was believed to have been intended for the common gardener.

**1586**: Sir Francis Drake brings sassafras and potatoes from America to England.

**1595**: Francis Bacon compiles lists of known garden flora and fauna.

**1606**: a Royal Charter established the Company of Gardeners; introduced by James I, it established the role of gardener as a recognised profession, 'the trade, crafte or mysterie of Gardening, planting, grafting, setting, sowing, cutting, arboring, rocking, mounting, covering, fencing and removing of plantes, herbes, seedes, fruites, trees, stocks, setts, and contriving the conveyances to the same.'

**1673**: Chelsea Physic Garden was founded, for the development of plants and their uses in medicine.

**1784**: seeds were sold in paper packets for the first time.

**1804**: the world-renowned Royal Horticultural Society was founded – a charity that promotes gardening and horticulture in Britain and Europe and organises the annual Chelsea Flower Show.

**1876**: Henry Wickham brought rubber tree seeds from Brazil to England.

**2000**: the Millennium Seed Bank was officially opened at Kew. Its aim is to have seeds from 25 per cent of the world's species of flora and fauna by 2020.

## The Gardener's Friend

*Now was there made fast y the touris wall*
*A garden fair, and in the corners set*
*An arbour green with wandis long and small*
*Railit about; and so with trieis set*
*Was all the place, and hawthorn hedges knet,*
*That life was non walking there forby*
*That might within scarse ony wight aspy.*

*So thick the bewis and the leaves green*
*Beshaded all the alleys that there were.*
*And myddis every arbour might be seen*
*The sharpe greene sweete juniper,*
*Growing so fair with branches here and there,*
*That – as it semed to a life without –*
*The bewis spread the arbour all about.*

*And on the smalle greene twistis sat*
*The little sweete nightingale, and song*
*So long and clear the ympnis consecrat*
*Of lufis use, now soft, now loud among,*
*That all the garden and the wallis rong*
*Right of their song, and of the copill next*
*Of their sweet harmony...*

JAMES I OF SCOTLAND (ATTRIBUTED), FROM *THE KINGIS QUAIR*

*All the wars of the world, all the Caesars, have not the staying power of a lily in a cottage garden.*

REGINALD FARRER

# Herb Gardens

*Those herbs which perfume the air most
delightfully, not passed by as the rest, but,
being trodden upon and crushed, are three;
that is, burnet, wild thyme and watermints.
Therefore, you are to set whole alleys of them,
to have the pleasure when you walk or tread.*

Francis Bacon, *Essays, Civil and Moral*

## HERBS TO GROW ON THE WINDOW SILL

Mint, sage, thyme, chives, lavender, rosemary, lemon balm, fennel, basil, dill, agrimony, coriander, oregano, parsley, bay, sorrel, sweet marjoram, lovage.

*Parsley – the jewel of herbs,*
*both in the pot and on the plate.*

ALBERT STOCKLI

# An Apothecary's Garden: Chelsea Physic Garden

Chelsea Physic Garden was established as an apothecaries' botanical garden in 1673. Its primary purpose was to train gardening apprentices and medical students in identifying plants, as well as to cultivate new plants from around the world. Some of these new plants would come to the garden through a seed-exchange scheme established with Leiden Botanical Gardens in the Netherlands in 1682. The plants were used in the manufacture of medicinal drugs in the laboratory at Apothecaries' Hall.

It remains today an important centre for natural medicine with its Garden of World Medicine and Pharmaceutical Garden. Its proximity to the Thames ensures a warmer microclimate, enabling non-native plants to thrive, including the largest outdoor fruiting olive tree in the country. It also boasts a Grade II listed rock garden, with rocks from places as diverse as the Tower of London and ballast used on Sir Joseph Banks' ship on an expedition to Iceland in 1772.

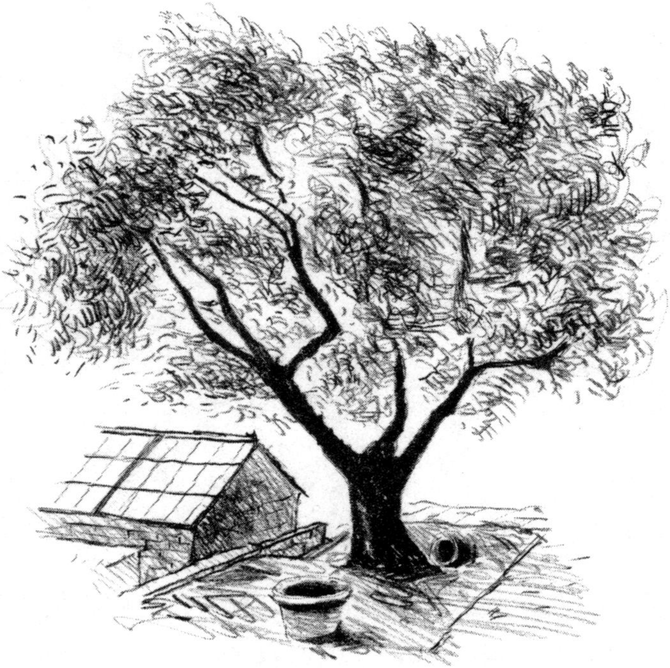

## Healing Herbs

Herbs are not only beneficial in healing human ailments, they can also be planted strategically in a garden to revitalise problematic soil or diseased plants. Revive unhealthy plants by planting chamomile next to them; comfrey will fertilise and cleanse tired soil by providing nitrogen and potassium.

*As for the garden of mint, the very smell of it alone recovers and refreshes our spirits, as the taste stirs up our appetite for meat.*

PLINY THE ELDER

## Gardeners' Tips – take care of yourself with herbs from the garden

**Sore feet** – if you've been on your feet all day, make up a basin or bucket of warm water, add in some lavender, sage or mint leaves and let your feet revive in the water for a few minutes.

**Sniffs and snuffles** – try inhaling an infusion of fresh rosemary or dried hollyhock flowers in boiling water, or drink tea containing fresh lemon balm leaves.

**Bad back** – apart from having a good stretch now and then when you're working in the garden, you could attempt the unusual cure of rubbing a cabbage leaf on the affected area. Alternatively, a more fragrant option is to gather a selection of strong-scented herbs, such as lavender and rosemary, and add these to oil; this can be sesame, almond, olive or even vegetable oil. Heat the oil and herbs on a low heat for five minutes, then leave to cool and add a few drops of essential oils if desired. Strain and decant the liquid into a dark-coloured glass bottle and get someone to massage the aches away.

*As for rosemary, I let it run all over my walls not only because my bees love it but because 'tis the herb sacred to remembrance.*

THOMAS MORE

*How vainly men themselves amaze,*
*To win the palm, the oak, or bays;*
*And their incessant labours see*
*Crowned from some single herb or tree.*

ANDREW MARVELL

# Famous Gardener: Nicolas Culpeper

Culpeper (1616–1654) was a gardener, apothecary and physician. As part of his apprentice training to become an apothecary, he would attend excursions led by Thomas Johnson, an assistant of the Apothecary Society and the editor of a new edition of *Gerard's Herbal*, published in 1633. He also developed a profound interest in astrology and was taken under the wing of William Lilly, a prominent and respected astrologer of the time. He eventually set up a practice in Spitalfields, London, as an astrologer and herbalist.

His book *The Complete Herbal* was published in 1653, and contains findings from his extensive cataloguing of medicinal herbs. He offered his skills as a physician free of charge to the public, almost unheard of at the time, and he would combine his knowledge of herbal remedies and astrology to treat his patients. His book *The English Physician* has been in print since the seventeenth century. It demonstrates to the layman how herbs and plants can be utilised in the treatment of all manner of illnesses; for example, burdock, when crushed and seasoned with salt, was recommended for dog bites, or if used internally it could help with flatulence. And bedstraw could be rubbed on the skin to stimulate blood clotting, or alternatively boiled in oil and taken internally to serve as an aphrodisiac. Culpeper's name lives on today as being synonymous with herbal products, partly due to the Culpeper Company founded by Hilda Leyel in 1927, which specialises in essential oils and aromatherapy products.

# Tree-mendous

*The true meaning of life is to plant trees, under whose shade you do not expect to sit.*

Nelson Henderson

*There are those who say that trees shade the garden too much, and interfere with the growth of the vegetables. There may be something in this: but when I go down the potato rows, the rays of the sun glancing upon my shining blade, the sweat pouring down my face, I should be grateful for shade.*

CHARLES DUDLEY WARNER

# A Weather Forecast from a Pine Cone

The pine cone is one of the most reliable natural weather indicators. In dry weather, pine cones open as the scales shrivel and stand out stiffly. When it is damp, they absorb moisture and, as the scales become flexible again, the cone returns to its normal shape. The cones are susceptible to dampness in the air long before the heavens open.

## Tree Folklore

**Oak** – the oak has long played an important role in British cultural beliefs and to this day it is considered unlucky to fell this king of the forest. Since the time of the Druids and right up until the mid seventeenth century, couples would have made their matrimonial vows under the naturally arched boughs of ancient oaks. Pagans carved the Green Man from oak and the traditional Yule log, used to provide warmth for the Christmas festivities, would also be oak. To find out the age of an oak tree, measure the circumference of the trunk approximately one and a half metres from the base. Take the measurement in centimetres and divide this number by 2.5; the result is the age of the tree. Oaks can survive for a millennium and grow upwards of 40 m high.

**Elder** – it is believed that wood from this species was used to make the cross upon which Christ was crucified, and witches are said to gather and shelter under the branches of elder trees. Elder wood is considered to be a conductor of magic and is used to make the 'Elder Wand' in the *Harry Potter* stories, the most powerful wand in the world of wizardry.

**Ash** – in Sussex, the ash is known as the 'Widow Maker', because large branches would often drop without prior warning. And in Norse mythology, the first man, Ask, was purported to have been carved from ash.

*Of all the trees that grow so fair,*
*Old England to adorn,*
*Greater is none beneath the sun,*
*Than Oak, and Ash, and Thorn.*
*Sing Oak, and Ash, and Thorn, good sirs,*
*(All of a Midsummer morn!)*
*Surely we sing of no little thing,*
*In Oak, and Ash, and Thorn!*

RUDYARD KIPLING, FROM 'A TREE SONG'

## Going Nuts

Many people have fond childhood memories of finding mahogany-coloured horse chestnuts among autumn leaves and stringing them up to do battle in the perennial playground favourite of conkers, or of roasting chestnuts and burning their fingers in the rush to eat them at Christmas time. Nut trees, given the right conditions, can be grown successfully in British gardens. Container-grown nut trees can be planted at any time of year, and bare-rooted saplings should be planted in autumn or spring. Here are some varieties that thrive in British gardens:

**Hazels** – this is one of the easiest nut trees to grow; they thrive in soils that are not too wet and not too dry and are best placed in a shady spot. Tiny red female flowers appear at the tips of the previous season's growth and these produce the nuts. The dull-yellow male catkins dangling from the branches are a lovely sight in the spring. As with fruit trees, it's best to plant in twos (or more) to allow cross-pollination, and they can be harvested in the autumn. Be aware that the flavour of the nuts will change once they are stored; newly harvested hazels have a crisp and under-ripe flavour, but after a few months in storage they reach their full crunchy nuttiness, just in time for Christmas.

**Sweet chestnuts** – these handsome trees require plenty of room, because they can grow up to 50 ft. They favour a warm, sunny spot. The wild varieties produce tiny nuts in their needle-sharp prickly cases, which aren't much use for roasting, so it's best to try an old variety, such as Marron de Lyon. This variety takes five years to produce its first crop. Newer varieties, such as Maraval, can be grown in containers and will crop after two seasons. Collect the chestnuts as soon as they fall from the tree, because they soon go mouldy on the ground. Make sure you wear gloves for this in case the cases haven't split. Preserve your harvest by blanching and peeling the nuts, then dry them and hang them up in netted bags. Chestnuts are very versatile and can be used for savoury and sweet dishes, including chocolate and chestnut cake, and they are a great addition to stuffing when roasting meats.

**Walnuts** – these can produce a crop even when planted in a small back garden, but this is one species that needs a mate to cross-pollinate because they are self-sterile. It is best to buy grafted trees from modern varieties, such as Lara and Fernette, which begin to bear fruit within three to four years. Walnuts, as with many nuts, are a rich natural source of calcium, potassium, manganese, selenium, vitamin B6, niacin and folate. They are also a great source of omega-3 fatty acids, which as well as helping to prevent heart disease may also guard against arthritis and other inflammatory diseases. In addition, walnuts are a good source of antioxidants and phytochemicals, which are thought to play important roles in reducing cholesterol levels and decreasing the risk of heart disease, cancer and other chronic diseases. It's best to harvest in June when the nuts are still green, otherwise the squirrels will do their best to pinch the lot. Store them by pickling them in fortified wine or vinegar.

*The tree which moves some to tears of joy is in the eyes of others only a green thing which stands in their way.*

WILLIAM BLAKE

*I never saw a discontented tree. They grip the ground as though they liked it, and though fast-rooted they travel about as far as we do. They go wandering forth in all directions with every wind, going and coming like ourselves, travelling with us around the sun two million miles a day, and through space heaven knows how fast and far!*

JOHN MUIR

## Tree-mendous

*I think that I shall never see*
*A poem lovely as a tree.*
*A tree whose hungry mouth is prest*
*Against the earth's sweet flowing breast;*
*A tree that looks at God all day*
*And lifts her leafy arms to pray;*
*A tree that may in Summer wear*
*A nest of robins in her hair;*
*Upon whose bosom snow has lain;*
*Who intimately lives with rain.*
*Poems are made by fools like me,*
*But only God can make a tree.*

JOYCE KILMER, 'TREES'

# When 'Hoe, Hoe, Hoe' is No Laughing Matter

*Many things grow in the garden that were never sown there.*

Thomas Fuller

## When 'Hoe, Hoe, Hoe' is No Laughing Matter

Weeds are often described as merely plants that are growing in the wrong place, but they are the bane of every gardener, and it doesn't seem to matter what you do in an attempt to destroy them; they will always reappear. There are three main types of weeds: grass-like weeds, grassy-type weeds and broadleaf weeds.

- ❀ Grass-like weeds closely resemble grass, but have triangular stems. These include wild garlic and Star of Bethlehem.

- ❀ Grassy-type weeds grow very much like the grass on our lawns and include crabgrass and foxtails.

- ❀ Broadleaf weeds are ubiquitous in British gardens. They have, as the name suggests, broad leaves and flowers, such as dandelions, clover and violets.

*Sweet flowers are slow and weeds make haste.*

WILLIAM SHAKESPEARE, *RICHARD III*

*Work is the crabgrass in the lawn of life.*

OLD ENGLISH PROVERB

# DANDELIONS

The common name for this rather attractive weed comes from the French *dent de lion*, which translates as 'lion's tooth'. The 'teeth' are the jagged green leaves. They have diuretic and laxative properties, which might have borne the old wives' tale that picking or even touching a dandelion will cause bed-wetting. The new leaves can, in fact, be eaten (without developing bladder problems) and make a great addition to salads and stir-fries.

During World War Two rationing, dandelion roots were dried and were commonly used as a substitute for coffee. The fruiting heads of the dandelion are popular with children as 'dandelion clocks', where the number of blows taken to remove the tufty white fruits is purported to tell the time; but, as discovered by Miles Kington, you shouldn't set your watch by them because 'the time always turns out to be 37 o'clock'!

*What we call a weed is in fact merely a plant growing where we do not want it.*

E. J. SALISBURY, *THE LIVING GARDEN*

## DAISIES

The daisy flowers throughout the year and appears en masse on many a British lawn. Described by Chaucer as the 'day's eye', its medicinal benefits are recorded in *Gerard's Herbal*, which dates from the sixteenth century. The leaves and flower heads were used in ointments and poultices to treat wounds, skin conditions and colds. These weeds, like dandelions, are also very popular with children as they can be made into daisy chains. In May 1985, villagers of Good Easter in Chelmsford made a record-breaking daisy chain that measured 1.31 miles. It took seven hours to complete!

# Red Clover

The leaves of this widespread plant, being either of the three-leaf or far rarer four-leaf variety, are more recognisable than the flowers. It is a herb that is used as a component in blood-thinning and hormone therapies. Of course, the four-leaf clover is famous because it is purported to bring good luck to those who find one. Richard Mabey, in his book *Flora Britannica*, claims that there are farms in America that have successfully grown four-leaf clovers using a genetically engineered secret ingredient, so that they can be sold as lucky charms in souvenir shops.

## When 'Hoe, Hoe, Hoe' is No Laughing Matter

*Brute force crushes many plants. Yet the plants rise again. The Pyramids will not last a moment compared with the daisy.*

D. H. Lawrence

*It gives one a sudden start in going down a barren, stony street, to see upon a narrow strip of grass, just within the iron fence, the radiant dandelion, shining in the grass, like a spark dropped from the sun.*

Henry Ward Beecher

## JAPANESE KNOTWEED

This species of weed is considered one of the most dangerous and invasive. It has hollow stems, which makes it look similar to bamboo. It can spread very quickly, damaging roads and building foundations and increasing the risk of flooding due to soil erosion. In 2010 a decision was made to release the Japanese psyllid insect into the wild in the UK as it feeds specifically on this weed.

Here are some of the most peculiar-sounding weeds that are common in British gardens: oxalis, ragwort, giant hogweed, sun spurge, goosegrass, speedwell, chickweed, fat hen, groundsel, shepherd's purse, hairy bittercress, willowherb, sow thistle, knotgrass.

## When 'Hoe, Hoe, Hoe' is No Laughing Matter

If you are a beginner who feels overwhelmed by the choice of gardening equipment, here are the basics you will need to get started:

- One short pointy thing for poking out weeds.
- One long pointy thing for poking out weeds when your back is sore.
- One small container for putting weeds in.
- One large container (e.g. a wheelie bin) for emptying the small container when it is full of weeds.
- A can of petrol to start a bonfire when your wheelie bin is full.

Michael Powell, *The Accidental Gardener: How to Create Your Own Tranquil Haven*

# Secret Gardens
# and Hidden Places

*Gardens... should be like lovely, well-shaped
girls: all curves, secret corners, unexpected
deviations, seductive surprises and
then still more curves.*

H. E. Bates, *A Love of Flowers*

Her allotment was a fairytale space. It was garlanded with bindweed's giant white flowers and festooned with brambles that bore glossy black berries and could wrap themselves around your ankle and rip your flesh to the bone. But if you looked hard enough, you could see that the seemingly forgotten space was sequinned with glorious islands of productivity: an autumn raspberry bed that offered sweet huge berries; a thicket of Jerusalem artichokes in which a horse could have disappeared from view; superb grafted fruit trees bearing velvety apricots or purple plums.

KAY SEXTON, *MINDING MY PEAS AND CUCUMBERS: QUIRKY TALES OF ALLOTMENT LIFE*

# Fairies at the Bottom of the Garden

In 1917 two young girls called Frances Griffiths and Elsie Wright produced some astonishing photographs of fairies dancing at the wooded beck at the bottom of their gardens. These photos were brought to the attention of *Sherlock Holmes*-writer Sir Arthur Conan Doyle and, being convinced that the photographs were genuine, he wrote about the 'Cottingley fairies' in a sold-out issue of *The Strand* in an article entitled 'An Epoch Making Event – Fairies Photographed'. Soon after this, Conan Doyle arranged for Geoffrey Hodson, a psychic, to interview the girls and visit the locations where the photographs were taken. Hodson reported back to Conan Doyle to say that he too had seen fairies dancing in the woods, and Doyle was convinced of their validity, which resulted in him publishing a book about the photographs called *The Coming of the Fairies* in 1922. It wasn't until nearly 70 years later, in the 1980s, that both Frances and Elsie admitted that the fairies in the photos were cardboard cut-outs.

It only tends to be small children that are taken in by this whimsical idea of other-worldly spirits inhabiting dark corners of gardens. Fairy rings are the closest a garden gets to fairy magic; these are rings of mushrooms or other fungi, that to a lawn lover are a bit of nuisance, which according to folklore

## Secret Gardens and Hidden Places

are gateways to fairy and elfin kingdoms that materialise when an elf or fairy comes into the garden. The elf is meant to return before the fairy ring disappears, so be on the look out, especially if you're planning on mowing the lawn!

... she held back the swinging curtain of ivy and pushed back the door which opened slowly... slowly.

Then she slipped through it, and shut it behind her, and stood with her back against it, looking about her and breathing quite fast with excitement, and wonder, and delight.

She was standing inside the secret garden.

It was the sweetest, most mysterious-looking place any one could imagine. The high walls which shut it in were covered with the leafless stems of climbing roses which were so thick that they were matted together. Mary Lennox knew they were roses because she had seen a great many roses in India. All the ground was covered with grass of a wintry brown and out of it grew clumps of bushes which were surely rose-bushes if they were alive. There were numbers of standard roses which had so spread their branches that they were like little trees. There were other trees in the garden, and one of the things which made the place look strangest and loveliest was that climbing roses had run all over them and swung down long tendrils which made light swaying curtains, and here and there they had caught at each other or at a far-reaching branch and bridges of themselves. There were neither leaves nor roses on them now and Mary did not know whether they were dead or alive, but their thin gray or brown branches and sprays looked like a sort of hazy mantle spreading over everything, walls, and trees, and even brown grass, where they had fallen from their fastenings and run along the ground. It was this hazy tangle from tree to tree which made it all look so mysterious. Mary had thought it must be different from other gardens which had not been left all by themselves so long; and indeed it was different from any other place she had ever seen in her life.

FRANCES HODGSON BURNETT, *THE SECRET GARDEN*

## Gardeners' Tips – creating a private space in your garden

Screen off sections of the garden with hedges, shrubs or rose- and ivy-strewn trellises to create private interconnecting 'rooms'. If your garden is small, an L-shape construction is sufficient to provide a secluded corner for a table and chairs.

For a larger garden, consider erecting a stone or concrete water feature with a partially hidden seating area.

An arbour at the bottom of the garden is another alternative. These are sheltered wooden seats, with climbing plants such as honeysuckle growing over them. These are most appealing places to relax after a hard day's toil in the garden, or simply to read the papers alfresco.

## Amazing Mazes

Garden labyrinths have long been synonymous with secret dalliances and illicit love affairs. It is alleged that in the mid twelfth century Henry II ordered a labyrinth to be built in his garden at Woodstock, so that he could conduct his affair with his mistress Rosamund without his wife Eleanor of Acquitane finding out. The French also developed labyrinths, which they called 'Houses of Daedalus', after the original labyrinth creator in Greek mythology who built an underground maze to house the Minotaur. Some labyrinths were made of box hedging but others incorporated staircases leading to subterranean tunnels.

Hedge mazes were a popular feature of noble and public gardens by the sixteenth century. They enabled people to meet socially and get some gentle exercise. Their popularity dwindled over the centuries because they were high maintenance. One of the oldest and most famous examples of the hedge maze is in the gardens of Hampton Court Palace. It was planted in 1702, during the reign of William III. If you were to walk the extent of the winding and twisting pathways you could end up walking well over half a mile, especially if you were to take a wrong turn! This particular maze is mentioned in Jerome. K. Jerome's *Three Men in a Boat*, when one of the three men becomes completely lost and meets other poor wanderers that he feared 'had given up all hope of ever seeing their home and friends again'.

*The green of the garden was greyed over with dew; indeed, all its colours were gone until the touch of sunrise.*

PHILIPPA PEARCE, *TOM'S MIDNIGHT GARDEN*

# GARDEN CREATURES GREAT AND SMALL

*I once had a sparrow alight upon my shoulder for a moment, while I was hoeing in a village garden, and I felt that I was more distinguished by that circumstance than I should have been by any epaulet I could have worn.*

HENRY DAVID THOREAU

*I value my garden more for being full of blackbirds than cherries, and very frankly give them fruit for their songs.*

JOSEPH ADDISON

*In our small pond by the front lawn, which is forested by lily pads and tall rushes, we have at least forty frogs and one corpulent toad that I've christened Johnny. They are my constant companions during the day, chirruping and croaking up at my open office window.*

ANNA NICHOLAS, *DONKEYS ON MY DOORSTEP*

## Gardeners' Tips – ways to attract wildlife back into the garden:

Make a simple rockery in a dark, damp corner, or choose dry-stone walls instead of fencing, as these make ideal habitats for small amphibians such as newts and frogs.

Leave some broken terracotta pots and rotting logs in dark corners of the garden as they make great homes for frogs and toads, as well as attracting beetles and other insects.

It is estimated that the number of house sparrows has declined by 68 per cent in the last 30 years due to the way that we manage our gardens. Tarmacking front gardens to accommodate vehicles and replacing hedging with fencing depletes their food and habitats, so consider these and other garden visitors before making any alterations.

Plant a bee-friendly garden with crocuses, snowdrops and heathers in spring, buddleia, thyme and lavender in the summer, flowering privet and ivy in winter.

*Behold the Frog, and then Contrast*
*His Present with his Humble Past!*
*Once but a Tadpole in a Pool,*
*Now nature's gayly Painted Fool.*
*So Newly Rich in Legs and Toes,*
*He's sadly lacking in Repose,*
*Yet He is never Impolite.*
*He hops and jumps from sheer delight,*
*And shows with each Gymnastic Spasm*
*The Convert's Fresh Enthusiasm.*

OLIVER HERFORD, 'THE FROG'

## The Dawn Chorus

Have you ever wondered what the birds are saying to each other as they sing out at sunrise? It's the male songbirds that practise their falsettos, and their calls can be interpreted as either 'Keep Away!' or 'Come Here Now!' The latter is a serenade to any females in earshot, to let them know that they have a territory of their own. The gaps in their love songs are so that they can listen for replies. The female birds fly to each territory to decide which is the best mate for them. The most successful males are those that can sing a loud and complex song, which, after a night of foraging, shows that he is a desirable mate. Some species of birds, notably the great tit and chaffinch, have an impressive repertoire of bird calls to make other males in the area believe that there are numerous birds around, and that all the territories are ear-marked – hence the 'Keep Away!' call.

# Make Fat Balls for Your Feathered Friends

Melt some lard in a saucepan. Once melted, allow to cool for a few minutes and mix in nuts, seeds, raisins, bacon rind, breadcrumbs and wild birdseed. Collect some yoghurt pots, carefully make a hole in the bottom of each one and thread a separate length of string through each and tie a knot at the bottom of the string. Fill the cartons with the lard mixture and place in the fridge to harden. Once the mixture has set, cut away the carton and hang the fat balls on branches and fences, but be sure that they are out of reach of predators.

## Top ten birds most commonly spotted in British gardens (according to the RSPB):

1. House sparrow
2. Starling
3. Blackbird
4. Blue tit
5. Chaffinch
6. Wood pigeon
7. Collared dove
8. Great tit
9. Robin
10. Long-tailed tit

# The Gardener's Friend

*Art thou the bird whom man loves best,*
*The pious bird with the scarlet breast,*
*Our little English Robin;*
*The bird that comes about our doors*
*When Autumn-winds are sobbing?*

William Wordsworth, from 'The Redbreast Chasing the Butterfly'

## Bird Folklore

**Robins** – these red-breasted birds are considered lucky. Wish upon the first robin you see in your garden in winter and your wish will come true – but only if the robin remains in your garden until you have finished saying your wish.

**Owl** – hearing an owl hooting during daylight hours portents that bad luck is on its way.

**Cuckoo** – the first call of the year from the cuckoo signals that spring is well on its way. Hearing a cuckoo's call on 14 April, also known as St Tiburtius' Day, you must turn over all the coins in your coat pockets while spitting and looking ahead, away from the ground – this unsavoury tradition will ensure good luck if you are standing on turf or soil, but bad luck if you are on a path.

## Food to Put Out to Encourage Other Visitors to the Garden:

Hedgehogs are great for diminishing the slug population. Put out a mixture of moist and dry dog food for them – never give them bread and milk as this plays havoc with their digestive system and can make them very ill.

Badgers favour unsalted peanuts and root vegetables. They also eat hedgehogs on occasion, so don't encourage both creatures into the garden at the same time.

Squirrels also like unsalted nuts and are partial to carrots and apples.

## Slippery Customers

The slow-worm is the most common reptile to be found in British gardens. They are non-venomous and are in fact lizards, having eyelids and a flat forked tongue. The males are grey brown and the females light brown with dark brown sides and a thin dark line down their backs. Provided you are not afraid of snake-like creatures, you can make them a habitat by piling up slate and stone in a dark, damp corner of the garden, perhaps near the compost heap. They are a popular visitor to gardens because they dine on slugs.

## Native Butterflies

There are around 59 species of butterfly in the UK, here are just a few that you might have the good fortune to spot in your garden: Peacock, Red Admiral, Cabbage White, Brimstone, Tortoiseshell, Comma, Painted Lady, Speckled Blue.

*Butterflies are self-propelled flowers.*

R. H. Heinlein

*Oh! Pleasant, pleasant were the days,
The time, when, in our childish plays,
My sister Emmeline and I
Together chased the butterfly!
A very hunter did I rush
Upon the prey: – with leaps and springs
I followed on from brake to bush;
But she, God love her, feared to brush
The dust from off its wings.*

WILLIAM WORDSWORTH, FROM 'TO A BUTTERFLY'

# The Hut Parade

*I saw something nasty in the woodshed!*

STELLA GIBBONS, ADA DOOM'S OFT-REPEATED LINE
IN *COLD COMFORT FARM*

# The Hut Parade

## Shed or 'Shud'

The word 'shed' is believed to have derived from 'shud', an Anglo-Saxon word for 'cover'. One definition from 1440 describes the shud as a 'hovel, swyne kote or howse of sympyl hyllynge to kepe yn beestys' – 'hyllynge' in this instance has been interpreted as 'covering'. It has been said that a shed is to a man what a handbag is to a woman – a private and reassuring place indelibly marked with the identity of its owner.

## Here Are Just a Few Reasons Why People Have Sheds:

Storing tools and garden supplies, keeping small family pets, fermenting beer, to work on reconditioning old motor vehicles, a private sanctuary, to house collections that the other half won't tolerate in the house, potting plants, hiding from the family, having children's tea parties, to write or paint a masterpiece. Some sheds have been transformed by their owners into saunas, cinemas for one, museums, and pubs with everything from beer pumps to plasma screens!

## LITERARY SHEDS

Philip Pullman, author of the successful *His Dark Materials* trilogy, writes in a shed at the bottom of the garden. Apart from having a comfortable chair to sit on and a desk and chair for working at his computer, it contains a six-foot-long stuffed rat, a saxophone and a guitar!

Roald Dahl famously wrote in his shed, which he regarded as his private sanctuary, where he could work without interruption. It was here that he wrote many of his most famous stories, such as *Charlie and the Chocolate Factory* and *James and the Giant Peach*.

Eighteenth-century man of letters William Cowper called his writer's shed his 'sulking room'.

Whilst living in Laugharne, West Wales, Dylan Thomas did his writing in his 'bard's bothy', an old boathouse. He would spend from two until seven o'clock in the 'wordsplashed hut' either writing, sleeping or looking out at the estuary below and the distant Gower, which provided inspiration for *Under Milk Wood*. His writer's hut or 'house on stilts high among the beaks and palavers of birds' is also where he wrote 'Poem on His Birthday' in 1949.

The 'Bard's Bothy'

# Gardeners' Tips – how to organise your shed

- Garden tools aren't cheap, so they need looking after. Hang up forks, spades, secateurs and hoes on the wall – keeping them away from the ground will stop them getting damp and rusty.

- Designate a folder or box for storing seed packets, use card dividers and write the name of the seed along with notes on their productivity etc.

- Hammer a few nails into the door or walls so that you can hang up your all-weather gardening gear.

## Tree Houses

Every child dreams of having a tree house in the garden, and some grown-ups do too. With visions of Swiss Family Robinson on their South Sea Island and the freedom of being up in the treetops, a tree house is a place to literally rise above everyday concerns. Tree houses have been built since the Middle Ages. The wealthy Medici family during the Italian Renaissance built a marble tree house. Modern tree houses are works of art; some are spherical and suspended from boughs like Christmas decorations, while others look like a pirate ship has become entangled in the branches. There is even a World Treehouse Association and an annual expo called Treesort in Oregon, USA.

## The Gardener's Friend

*Here, free from riot's hated noise,*
*Be mine, ye calmer, purer joys,*
*A book or friend bestows;*
*Far from the storms that shake the great,*
*Contentment's gale shall fan my seat,*
*And sweeten my repose.*

William Cowper, 'For a Moss-House in the
Shrubbery at Weston'

*The Sun* newspaper conducted a poll to discover how much time the average male spent in his shed. Their findings revealed that the time spent was three hours and twenty minutes per week. They went on to calculate how much time they would spend in their sheds in a lifetime and concluded that it 'works out to more than seven days a year and between the ages of 30 and 76 a total of 11 months.' They also found out that 'one in ten have stuck a sofa and television in there'!

# GREEN PASTURES

*Nothing is more pleasant to the eye than green grass kept finely shorn.*

FRANCIS BACON

# History of the English Lawn

The quintessential English lawn first appeared in gardens in the early 1600s. It was a sign of high status among the Jacobean gentry to own an immaculate lawn, because only the wealthiest had the means to maintain one. These lawns would be hand-sheared or scythed to give a perfect finish, as it was not until 1830 that the first mower was invented – and so began man's obsession for the perfect turf.

With the development of the mower, lawns were no longer the preserve of the rich and became a common feature of gardens. Victorians in particular made use of their immaculate lawns with games and sports, such as cricket, bowls, croquet and tennis.

The Garden Club of America, in an attempt to keep up with its transatlantic neighbours in the early twentieth century, insisted that its followers maintained 'a plot with a single type of grass with no intruding weeds, kept mown at a height of an inch and a half, uniformly green and neatly edged'. But the lawn thrives in the English drizzle, which was emulated on American lawns with the introduction of the sprinkler.

Many of today's lawns are being replaced with more useful crops; even Michelle Obama has ploughed up the White House lawn to grow organic vegetables.

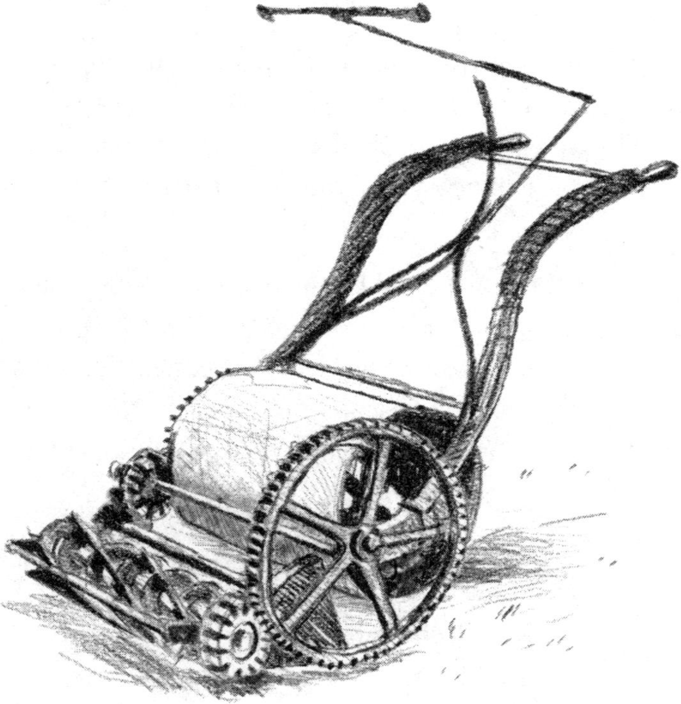

## Gardeners' Tips – lawn maintenance

- Remove weeds without weedkiller, as this can be harmful to pets, by digging the offenders out with a knife or narrow-bladed trowel. Try to dig out the roots to prevent regrowth, but avoid disturbing the lawn too much.

- Molehills are a real blot on the landscape. A humane method of sending moles packing is to plant glass bottles (without lids on) into the molehills with the top of the bottle showing, so that the noise of the wind travels through their tunnels, encouraging them to move to a more peaceful location.

- Water your lawn during dry spells in spring and summer. You may need to water it as often as twice a week in the height of summer. Make your own sprinkler by recycling an old garden hose. Once it has sprung a few leaks, simply make a few more holes with a sharp nail and voila!

## Green Pastures

❀ Don't throw away grass cuttings; left on the lawn they will provide up to a quarter of your lawn's fertiliser requirements. This nutrient-rich fodder contains around 1 per cent phosphorus, 2 per cent potassium and 4 per cent nitrogen, and while it breaks down it serves as a food source for the soil's bacteria, which are vital for healthy turf.

*A perfect summer day is when the sun is shining, the breeze is blowing, the birds are singing and the lawnmower is broken.*

James Dent

*Grass is the cheapest plant to install and the most expensive to maintain.*

Pat Howell

*The original Garden of Eden could not have had such turf as one sees in England.*

Charles Dudley Warner, *My Summer in a Garden*

# Heaven on Earth

*What do gardeners do when they retire?*

BOB MONKHOUSE

# An Inspirational Garden: Derek Jarman's Garden in Dungeness, Kent

The late Derek Jarman was an art house film-maker and photographer. He was also the creator of a unique garden on the shingle spit at Dungeness, a place that many would regard as bleak and desolate, with its nuclear power station whirring in the distance and scattering of single-storey chalet-style buildings. He stumbled upon the spot while searching for bluebell woods to film on his Super-8 camera.

He applied his artist's eye and horticultural expertise to create the garden, which combined flints, pebbles and driftwood with the area's indigenous plants, shrubs and flowers. Beginning with monoliths made of knuckles of salvaged bone that were used to train dog roses, he went on to develop raised herb beds which were edged with scallop shells, and ragged flints were used to protect new plants from careless feet. The overall effect is like that of a wild, sensory garden, with its standing stones, shingle raked into concentric circles and beach-finds carefully arranged into sculptural pieces, with hardy gorse and low-level, seaside-loving plants. It's an extraordinary sight; an oasis on the shingle. Of his garden he once said, 'Paradise haunts gardens, and it haunts mine.'

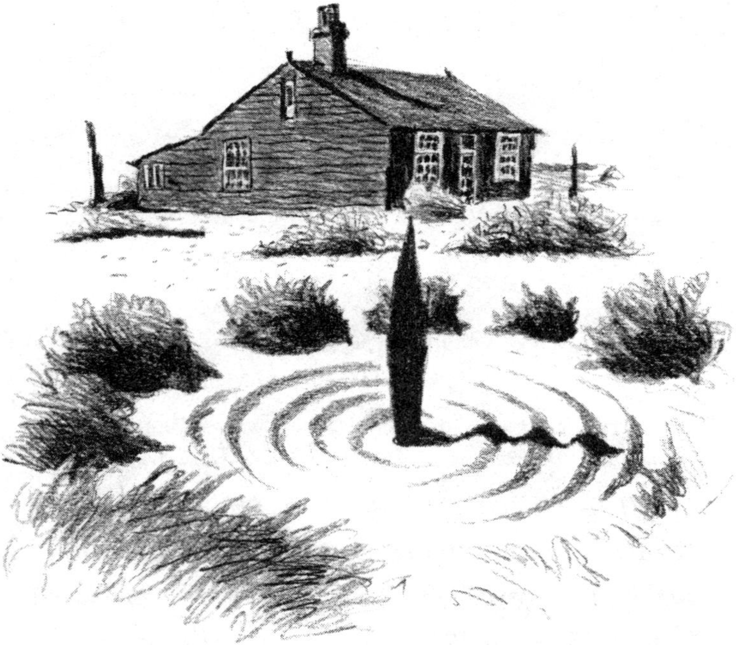

*When your garden is finished I hope it will be more beautiful than you anticipated, require less care than you expected, and have cost only a little more than you had planned.*

Thomas D. Church

*And he gave it for his opinion that whoever could make two ears of corn, or two blades of grass, to grow upon a spot of ground where only one grew before, would deserve better of mankind, and do more essential service to his country, than the whole race of politicians put together.*

Jonathan Swift, *Gulliver's Travels*

# Gardeners' Tips – protecting your patch of heaven

- ❀ 'Season' your garden with black pepper to discourage cats from using it as an outside toilet.

- ❀ Use leftover water from a recently boiled kettle to kill off cabbage worms by pouring it over your crops.

- ❀ Make bird-scarers by upending brightly coloured plastic drinks bottles on garden canes and planting them in the soil amongst your crops.

- ❀ Slugs are the bane of gardeners and there are various methods to try to eradicate them:

    – sprinkle coffee grounds around your plants; the coffee is believed to dry up the slugs.
    – pour beer into saucers and place around the garden, as slugs are well known to enjoy a tipple and with luck they will topple over into the amber liquid.

# Famous Gardener: Harold Peto

Harold Peto (1854–1933) was the son of a wealthy engineer and railway magnate, and grew up at Sommerleyton Hall in Suffolk. He trained as an architect and ran a practice for 21 years. The city life, however, did not satisfy, and he switched careers in favour of a quieter life in the country, where he could indulge his growing interest in landscape and garden design. One of his first commissions was to redesign Easton Lodge, East Anglia, where he utilised his architectural skills by creating formal balustrades, stone columns and terraces in an Italian/French style that, surprisingly, looked completely in keeping with the rolling British countryside. Other notable features are a tree house in an avenue lined with lime trees and a Japanese garden inspired by his visit to the Far East in 1898. The Edwardian era heralded a golden age, and Peto's style did not simply reflect this, it set the precedent. His other works can be found at West Dean Gardens, Garinish Island, County Cork, and at his home Iford Manor, Wiltshire, among many other commissions.

*If I'm ever reborn, I want to be a gardener – there's too much to do for one lifetime!*

KARL FOERSTER

# Exotic Gardens

*These gardens are created for rest in cool surroundings, for idleness and sauntering and imaginative thought.*

Osbert Sitwell on exotic gardens

# The Hanging Gardens of Babylon

This garden, built around 600 BC, has long since disappeared. It is believed to have been a gift from King Nebuchadnezzar to his wife, who was missing the flora and fauna of her Persian homeland. Descriptions of the gardens by ancient Greek historians are all that is left of this wonder of the ancient world. Philo gives this description:

'The Hanging Garden has plants cultivated above ground level, and the roots of the trees are embedded in an upper terrace rather than in the earth. The whole mass is supported on stone columns... Streams of water emerging from elevated sources flow down sloping channels... These waters irrigate the whole garden saturating the roots of plants and keeping the whole area moist. Hence the grass is permanently green and the leaves of trees grow firmly attached to supple branches... This is a work of art, of royal luxury, and its most striking feature is that the labour of cultivation is suspended above the heads of the spectators.'

## Gardeners' Tips – exotic plants to grow in your garden

**Yucca** – with their sword-like evergreen foliage, these plants make a dramatic focal point in a garden. Plant container-grown yuccas in spring in a sunny spot, and allow plenty of space because they can grow to two metres.

**Palm trees** – these fronded trees are a common sight in British gardens and are perfect for the increased incidence of summer drought. The best palm for hardiness is the Chusan Palm from China, which has large, fan-shaped leaves on the top of a spectacular hairy trunk. If fed and watered well it can grow to a height of between 18 and 21 ft (6–7 m), but if your garden is small there is a miniature version available which reaches a more comfortable 12–15 ft (4–5 m).

**Banana** – provided these plants are given adequate protection through the winter, bananas should survive the British weather and reward you with a harvest. A straw coat will protect the trunk from freezing temperatures. There are a number of varieties to try, from Musa basjoo to the rather wonderful-sounding Ensete superbum!

*Before entering the old property, we look out onto the sprawling Mediterranean garden. Bursting with oranges and lemons and backed by grizzled mountains, it ushers the visitor back to a time when Graves, in old straw hat and peasant shirt, picked his own bitter oranges to make marmalade.*

Anna Nicholas, *Donkeys on My Doorstep*
Describing the gardens of Ca N'Alluny, the Mallorcan home of the late Robert Graves

## Unique Gardens of the World

**Las Pozas, Xilitla, Mexico** – this surreal garden was devised by eccentric British philanthropist Edward James after he commented that he wanted 'a Garden of Eden'. It contains numerous follies with names like 'The House with the Roof like a Whale, and a 'Staircase to Heaven', small buildings that used to house James' extensive menagerie of exotic animals and birds, and sculptures up to four-stories high of popular surrealist themes such as spiral staircases winding their way up to the treetops.

**Kirstenbosch, Cape Town, South Africa** – owned at one time by Cecil Rhodes, who bequeathed it on his death to the government, this botanical garden on the eastern slopes of Table Mountain is an important conservation centre and home to thousands of rare indigenous plants. Friendly guinea fowl stalk the grounds.

**The Rock Garden of Chandigarh, India** – this staggering sculptural garden belies its humble origins. It was started nearly four decades ago by Nek Chand, an ordinary man who, after clocking-off each evening from his job working as a transport official, would make his way to the jungle on the edge of the town where, under cover of darkness, for fear of being caught by government authorities, he set about making himself a rock and sculpture garden. It started with a few figures made out of discarded materials and grew over the years into several acres' worth of mosaic courtyards containing figures. When the authorities did eventually catch up with him, rather than punishing him they gave him the means (a salary and a workforce) to continue his artful creation. It now extends to 25 acres and is considered one of the wonders of the modern world, receiving 5,000 visitors daily.

**Lucullus, Rome, Italy** – this legendary garden, situated above the Spanish Steps, was the place where early European horticulturalists made there first attempts to 'tame nature' in the first century BC. Lucullus was an army general who oversaw campaigns in Asia Minor. It was during his time in Mesopotamia and Persia that he developed his interest in gardens, and he funded his Roman garden from 'the spoils of the barbarians'. He is believed to have introduced cherries and apricots to the West. His gardens became a benchmark for all the pleasure gardens in Rome. Mosaics have recently been excavated at Lucullus, showing a cupid riding a dolphin and a wolf's head in green and gold.

## Exotic Gardens

**Monet's Garden, Giverny, France** – in this rapturous garden you are literally walking into some of Monet's finest works. The Japanese bridge that strides the lake containing his water lilies and rowing boat, the iron archways of climbing roses and banks of wild and rare flowers that Monet liked to mix together can all be found here. He would plant flowers according to colour and allow them to grow freely and unconstrained.

## The Gardener's Friend

He had been visiting a friend in a neighbouring country, and that friend having recently had his grounds laid out by an improver, Mr Rushworth was returned with his head full of the subject, and very eager to be improving his own space in the same way...

'I must try to do something with it,' said Mr Rushworth, 'but I do not know what. I hope I shall have some good friend to help me.'

'Your best friend upon such as occasion,' said Miss Bertram, calmly, 'would be Mr Repton, I imagine.'

'That is what I was thinking of. As he has done so well by Smith, I think I had better have him at once. His terms are five guineas a day.'

**Jane Austen, *Mansfield Park***

# A Year in the Garden

*The gardening season officially begins on January 1st and ends on December 31st.*

Marie Huston

# A Brief Guide to the Gardener's Year

**January** – go through your garden tools, sharpen secateurs, sweep out the shed, order in seeds. Keep off the frozen grass because this will cause long-term damage, and be careful not to trample on green shoots and early snowdrops and crocuses. If the snow comes be sure not to let it rest on bushes and trees, because the extra weight can cause bushes to topple over and branches to break. Remember your feathered friends during this cold, dark month and put out fat balls, kitchen scraps and keep the bird bath, or an upturned bin lid, topped up with fresh water.

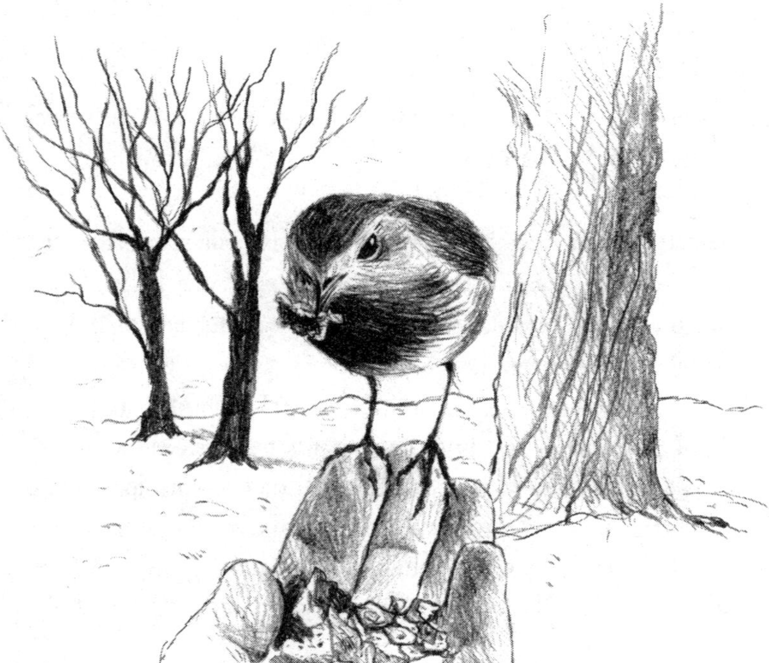

**February** – plant bare-rooted roses and clematis. Rake gravel paths to remove weeds.

**March** – plant seeds into borders and place potted narcissi that are now past their best into a sunny spot, with bulbs 10 cm down. Aphids are waking up, so be ready for them with a spray bottle full of soapy water.

**April** – remove weeds from your flower beds, put out hanging baskets and potted flowers. Sow annuals such as cornflowers and nasturtiums. Plant carrot and Swiss chard, courgette seeds in the vegetable patch, sow pumpkins in pots but keep these indoors. Give the lawn its first mow of the year, and clear the compost bin.

*On the first day of spring, I dig my fingers deep into the soft earth. I can feel its energy, and my spirits soar.*

**HELEN HAYES**

## The Gardener's Friend

*I love spring anywhere, but if I could choose
I would always greet it in a garden.*

RUTH STOUT

*In the spring, at the end of the day,
you should smell like dirt.*

MARGARET ATWOOD

# A Year in the Garden

**May** – plant your container-grown trees and shrubs in the garden. Plant runner beans, swede and sweetcorn in the vegetable patch. Dispense with greenfly by squashing them between your fingers. Plant out your hanging baskets. Be on the lookout for weed seedlings and dig these up regularly.

**June** – protect your burgeoning fruit plants from birds by stringing up a home-made bird-scarer made from unwanted shiny objects, such as old cutlery, CDs and foil cases, strung together with twine. Place container-grown citrus trees outside in the sun, deadhead the roses, unless you want an autumn display of rosehips, and take cuttings from pinks. Sow hardy biennials now.

**July** – cut back spent flower stems. Sow turnips, winter radishes and lamb's lettuce, and harvest onions. Pick your summer-fruiting crops, such as raspberries, strawberries and currants.

**August** – ask a friendly neighbour to water the garden, and top up the pond – if you have one – if you are going on holiday during the summer. Harvest aubergines and other ripe fruits and vegetables.

## The Gardener's Friend

*Bulb: potential flower buried in autumn,
never to be seen again.*

Henry Beard

*I cannot endure to waste anything as precious
as autumn sunshine by staying in the house.
So I spend almost all the daylight
hours in the open air.*

Nathaniel Hawthorne

*Delicious autumn! My very soul is wedded to it, and if I were a bird I would fly about the earth seeking the successive autumns.*

GEORGE ELIOT

**September** – plant hyacinth bulbs for Christmas, and plant spring-flowering biennials and spring bulbs, such as crocus and narcissus.

**October** – rake the autumn leaves off the lawn to prevent the grass from yellowing, and burn diseased leaves so that they don't infect other parts of the garden. Plant soft fruit bushes.

**November** – if you've built a bonfire for Guy Fawkes' Night, carefully check that no small creatures have set up home before lighting it. Prune back soft fruit trees. Move container plants to a sheltered spot for winter. Clear moss from pathways, because this can become treacherous when wet.

**December** – remove worm casts on the lawn with a stiff brush. Check stored fruit for rot and disease. Cut back creepers, especially ones that climb house walls, so that leaves don't gather in the guttering.

# A Year in the Garden

*Every gardener knows that under the cloak of winter lies a miracle... a seed waiting to sprout, a bulb opening to the light, a bud straining to unfurl.*

Barbara Winkler

# Garden Festivals

The Garden Tourism Festival (India) – February

Canada Blooms (Canada) – March

The Sydney Garden and Flower Show (Australia) – April

Chaumont International Garden Festival (France) – April to October

RHS Chelsea Flower Show (UK) – May

Gardening Scotland (Edinburgh, UK) – May

Chilli Fiesta (West Sussex, UK) – June

BBC Gardener's World Live (Birmingham, UK) – June

RHS Hampton Court Palace Flower Show (UK) – July

The Singapore Garden Festival – July (biennial)

Canterbury in Bloom Gardener's Festival (Kent, UK) – October

*There ought to be gardens for all the months in the year, in which, severally, things of beauty may be then in season.*

FRANCIS BACON

# A Gardener's Life

*The love of gardening is a seed once sown that never dies.*

GERTRUDE JEKYLL

## A Gardener's Life

*My garden will never make me famous,
I'm a horticultural ignoramus.*

OGDEN NASH

*Kind hearts are the gardens,
Kind thoughts are the roots,
Kind words are the flowers,
Kind deeds are the fruits.
Take care of your garden
And keep out the weeds,
Fill it with sunshine,
Kind words and kind deeds.*

HENRY WADSWORTH LONGFELLOW

*Mr Collins invited them to take a stroll in the garden, which was large and well laid out, and to the cultivation of which he attended himself. To work in his garden was one of his most respectable pleasures.*

JANE AUSTEN, *PRIDE AND PREJUDICE*

*You must not know too much or be too precise or scientific about birds and trees and flowers and watercraft; a certain free-margin, and even vagueness – ignorance, credulity – helps your enjoyment of these things.*

HENRY DAVID THOREAU

*No occupation is so delightful to me as the culture of the earth, no culture comparable to that of the garden.*

THOMAS JEFFERSON

*Who has learned to garden who did not at the same time learn to be patient?*

H. L. V. FLETCHER

# Famous Gardener: Lancelot 'Capability' Brown

Lancelot Brown (1716–1783) began his working life as a gardener's boy at Kirkharle Hall, Northumberland. He quickly climbed the ranks and moved to Stowe Park, Buckinghamshire, to join the gardening team there, under the tutelage of the great landscape architect William Kent. During this period Kent inspired him to take the trend of 'natural gardening' to a whole new level – using simple water features and open expanses, he aimed to recreate a sense of the untouched about the British landscape.

His first opportunity to display his skill for 'perfecting nature' came when he was commissioned to landscape the Duke of

Grafton's Wakefield estate. These became known as the 'serpentine' gardens, after he replaced the estate's Renaissance style with a sweeping landscape of lakes, grassy parkland and woodland.

Over the coming years his reputation led him to transform some of the most famous gardens in England, including those at Hampton Court, Chatsworth and Blenheim Palace. It was around this time that he earned the nickname 'Capability', after his frequent declaration that English estates had 'great capability for improvement'. So determined was he to perfect the nation's gardens that, on receiving an Irish commission, he refused on the grounds that he had not yet 'finished' England.

Brown dedicated so much of his life to the imitation of nature that on his death Horace Walpole famously wrote to Lady Ossory: 'Your dryads must go into black gloves, Madam, their father-in-law, Lady Nature's second husband, is dead!'

*To dig one's own spade into one's own earth! Has life anything better to offer than this?*

JOHN BEVERLEY NICHOLS

# A Gardener's Life

*Beastly garden!*

VITA SACKVILLE-WEST WHEN THINGS DIDN'T QUITE GO AS PLANNED

*The longer I live the greater is my respect and affection for manure...*

ELIZABETH VON ARNIM

## The Gardener's Friend

*If you think 'hoe hoe' is a laughing matter, you're no gardener.*

HERBERT V. PROCHNOW

*What a man needs in gardening is a cast-iron back with a hinge on it.*

CHARLES DUDLEY WARNER, *MY SUMMER IN A GARDEN*

# A Gardener's Life

*In his garden every man may be his own artist without apology or explanation.*

LOUISE BEEBE WILDER

## THE GARDENER'S FRIEND

*The gardener does not love to talk,*
*He makes me keep the gravel walk;*
*And when he puts his tools away,*
*He locks the door and takes the key.*

*Away behind the currant row*
*Where no one else but cook may go,*
*Far in the plots, I see him dig*
*Old and serious, brown and big.*

*He digs the flowers, green, red and blue,*
*Nor wishes to be spoken to.*
*He digs the flowers and cuts the hay,*
*And never seems to want to play.*

*Silly gardener! Summer goes,*
*And winter comes with pinching toes,*
*When in the garden bare and brown*
*You must lay your barrow down.*

*Well now, and while the summer stays*
*To profit by these garden days*
*O how much wiser you would be*
*To play at Indian wars with me!*

ROBERT LOUIS STEVENSON, 'THE GARDENER'

# Resources

## WEBSITES:

www.bbc.co.uk/gardenersworld

www.eatweeds.co.uk

www.kew.org

www.shedman.co.uk

www.telegraph.co.uk/gardening

www.theflowerexpert.com

## PUBLICATIONS:

Binney, Ruth *Wise Words and Country Ways for Gardeners* (2007, David & Charles)

Brook, Jane *Gardening Wit* (2009, Summersdale Publishers)

Brown, Jane *The Pursuit of Paradise: A Social History of Gardens and Gardening* (1999, HarperCollins)

Carlson, Isobel *Trugs, Dibbers, Trowels and Twine* (2010, Summersdale Publishers)

Clevely, A. M. *Your Kitchen Garden: Month by Month* (2010, David & Charles)

*Country Life* magazine

Eastoe, Jane *Wild Food: Foraging for Food in the Wild* (2008, Anova)

Harrison, Lorraine *20 Sussex Gardens* (2007, Snake River Press)

Hodgson Burnett, Frances *The Secret Garden* (1911)

Holden, Edith *The Country Diary of an Edwardian Lady* (1977, Michael Joseph Ltd)

## Resources

Lacey, Stephen *Gardens of the National Trust* (1996, National Trust Enterprises)

McGovern, Una *Lost Crafts: Rediscovering Traditional Skills* (2008, Chambers)

Musgrave, Toby *The Head Gardeners: Heroes of Horticulture* (2007, Aurum Press Ltd)

Pevsner, Nicholas *Garden Buildings of England*

Powell, Michael *The Accidental Gardener* (2004, Summersdale Publishers)

Sexton, Kay *Minding My Peas and Cucumbers: Quirky Tales of Allotment Life* (2011, Summersdale Publishers)

Struthers, Jane *Red Sky at Night* (2009, Ebury Press)

*The English Garden* magazine

Titchmarsh, Alan *The Kitchen Garden: Grow Your Own Fruit and Veg* (2008, BBC Books)

Uglow, Jenny *A Little History of British Gardening* (2004, Chatto & Windus)

www.summersdale.com